ADVANCE PRAISE FOR
The Changing Shape of Our Salvation

A solid piece of scholarly research into a very important and grossly overlooked cornerstone of every religion and denomination. In following the train of the book's thought I learned to appreciate even more the author's carefully developed insights into a subject that is not open to easy analysis. The concept of salvation is not a matter that can be treated lightly because it affects the basic beliefs of those committed to their faith, regardless of their religion or denomination. I hope theologians and scripture scholars as well as thoughtful religious lay people of all religions will ponder what is so thoughtfully offered to them is this small but precious volume.

— **Fr. Joseph F. Girzone,** author of the bestselling Joshua books

Dr. John Killinger begins this wise and readable book about salvation with a shrewd assessment of the varied understandings of salvation in the Old and New Testaments. He follows this up with an overview of understandings of salvation through the history of the church, and he concludes the book with a refreshing and provocative survey of contemporary understandings of salvation. He probes contested issues with the engaging candor which readers of his earlier books have come to expect from him. The book is both a mirror in which readers may view the gift of salvation that is within them and a window through which they may view the God who in love has saved them. It is, like its author, both charming and inspiring, and I recommend it enthusiastically.

— **Fisher H. Humphreys,** author and
Professor of Divinity, Beeson Divinity School

The Changing Shape of Our Salvation is a timely theological look at the question of salvation which will enable pastors to confront the pop culture theology promoted by many media evangelists. In a day when so many pastors merely follow the lead of the pop culture, John Killinger uses sound hermeneutics to address the question of salvation. Every pastor who wants to address post-modern concerns and give their people sound theological understanding of the Judeo-Christian view of salvation will want this commentary in their library.

– **Rev. Donald Colhour,** Senior Minister,
Wilshire Christian Church, Los Angeles

John Killinger is at it again — challenging stereotypes, expanding minds, opening hearts, enflaming imaginations, and evoking gratitude. In his book, Killinger leads us through a careful examination of the subject of salvation in Holy Scripture and ecclesiastical tradition into the surprise and excitement of the experience of salvation in a new religious world vibrant with the possibilities of shared meaning and fulfillment in a truly inclusive community.

Killinger provides his readers with a sound primer on the subject of salvation that becomes a powerful prod, catching us by surprise and catapulting us into a religious world as welcome as it is new.

In a world of volatile religious diversity, John Killinger summons us to an understanding of the spiritual meaning of salvation in Christianity that, if embraced, can serve as a catalyst for our personal contributions to the physical reality of salvation in joyful fellowship with one another.

– **C. Welton Gaddy,** Pastor for Preaching and Worship,
Northminster Baptist Church, Monroe, Louisiana,
and President, The Interfaith Alliance

THE CHANGING SHAPE
— OF —
OUR SALVATION

OTHER BOOKS BY THE AUTHOR

Seven Things They Don't Teach You in Seminary (Crossroad, 2006)

Winter Soulstice: Celebrating the Spirituality of the Wisdom Years (Crossroad, 2005)

God, the Devil, and Harry Potter: A Christian Minister's Defense of the Beloved Novels (St. Martin's, 2002)

Ten Things I Learned Wrong from a Conservative Church (Crossroad, 2002)

Lost in Wonder, Love, and Praise: Prayers and Affirmations for Christian Worship (Abingdon, 2001)

Preaching the New Millennium (Abingdon, 1999)

Raising Your Spiritual Awareness Through 365 Simple Gifts from God (Abingdon, 1998)

The Night Jessie Sang at the Opry (Angel Books, 1996)

Preaching to a Church in Crisis: A Homiletic for the Last Days of the Mainline Church (CSS, 1996)

Day by Day with Jesus: A Devotional Commentary on the Four Gospels (Abingdon, 1994)

Jessie: A Novel (McCracken, 1993)

Beginning Prayer (Upper Room, 1993)

Letting God Bless You: The Beatitudes for Today (Abingdon, 1992)

You Are What You Believe: The Apostles' Creed for Today (Abingdon, 1990)

Christmas Spoken Here (Broadman, 1989)

To My People with Love: The Ten Commandments for Today (Abingdon, 1988)

The God Named Hallowed: The Lord's Prayer for Today (Abingdon, 1987)

Christ and the Seasons of Marriage (Broadman, 1987)

Parables for Christmas (Abingdon, 1985)

Fundamentals of Preaching (Fortress, 1985; SCM, 1986; rev. 1998)

Christ in the Seasons of Ministry (Word, 1983)

The Loneliness of Children (Vanguard, 1980; Éditions Robert Laffont, 1983)

His Power in You (Doubleday, 1978)

A Sense of His Presence (Doubleday, 1977)

Bread for the Wilderness, Wine for the Journey (Word, 1976)

The Salvation Tree (Harper & Row, 1973)

World in Collapse: The Vision of Absurd Drama (Dell, 1973)

The Fragile Presence: Transcendence in Contemporary Literature (Fortress, 1973)

Leave It to the Spirit: Freedom and Responsibility in the New Liturgies (Harper & Row, 1971)

For God's Sake, Be Human (Word, 1970)

The Failure of Theology in Modern Literature (Abingdon, 1965)

Hemingway and the Dead Gods (University Press of Kentucky, 1960; Citadel, 1965)

THE CHANGING SHAPE
——— OF ———
OUR SALVATION

JOHN KILLINGER

A *Crossroad* Book
The Crossroad Publishing Company
New York

The Crossroad Publishing Company
16 Penn Plaza – 481 Eighth Avenue, Suite 1550
New York, NY 10001

Printed in the United States of America on acid-free paper

The text of this book is set in 11/16 Goudy Old Style. The display faces are Goudy Handtooled and Serlio.

Library of Congress Cataloging-in-Publication Data
Killinger, John.
     The changing shape of our salvation / John Killinger.
          p.   cm.
     ISBN-13: 978-0-8245-2422-7 (alk. paper)
     ISBN-10: 0-8245-2422-5 (alk. paper)
     1. Salvation – Christianity – History of doctrines.   2. Future life –
History of doctrines.   3. Eternity – History of doctrines.   I. Title.
     BT751.3.K55 2006
     234.09 – dc22
                                                                 2006035302

1 2 3 4 5 6 7 8 9 10   13 12 11 10 09 08 07

For my dear friend in life and ministry

Walter J. Vernon

whose absolute faith in his salvation
when he was handed a possible death sentence
gave me renewed confidence
in my own

Contents

Introduction

During 1972–1973, I served on a committee of the National Council of Churches chaired by the Rev. Dr. David Randolph of the United Methodist Board of Discipleship in Nashville, Tennessee. The committee was charged with studying the meaning of salvation in the modern world. The plan was for our committee to deliberate on the subject for a year, then send our conclusions on to the World Council of Churches, where they would form the basis for further discussions at a great international plenary session.

We had three or four committee meetings, at which various papers were presented and we talked at length. Then, in June 1973, a month or so before the World Council meeting, our committee met in its final session at Rehoboth Beach, Delaware. In addition to the usual theologians and pastors, Dr. Randolph had invited a number of extra persons to attend this session, including a bold-hearted contemporary artist from Florida State University named Walter Gaudnek.

During one of the afternoon sessions of this meeting, it was announced that we were to repair to a certain dock, where Gaudnek would be in charge of a "happening." (Happenings were all the rage at the time.) What Gaudnek had planned for our happening was that the members of our group would man several small dinghies and row them out into the harbor. Then, circling clockwise, we would hold aloft several signs or banners he had prepared for the occasion, all pertaining to the subject of salvation. Gaudnek himself would remain on the dock, directing and videotaping the happening.

There were two things he had not anticipated. One was that there were no experienced rowers in our group and maneuvering the dinghies was not as easy a feat as it might sound. The other was that the coast was just then being struck by gale-force winds in advance of Hurricane Agnes, and the winds were kicking up three- and four-foot waves inside the harbor.

Our whole attempt was a farce.

"Keep the boats in a circle!" shouted Gaudnek, to little avail. "Get those signs in the air!" One man actually fell out of his boat and nearly drowned before his companions could rescue him.

Some of the old salts sitting around the dock laughed at us until their sides hurt. It was clear that they had never seen anything like us greenhorns trying to be sailors.

Following that comical episode, Gaudnek directed us to get into cars and follow him down the coast. There, he had found a dilapidated old sea shanty and obtained permission for us to paint it. For that purpose, he had brought along in the back of his station wagon several dozen cans or half-cans of paint, none of whose contents matched the colors in the others, and a shopping bag full of brushes and rollers. He had also arranged for a saxophonist named Ed Summerlin, who taught jazz at the Eastman

School of Music in Rochester, New York, to play while we were working and for a middle-aged terpsichorist attired in a black leotard to do interpretive dancing on the large boulders along the ocean.

Our group spread out over the shanty, some even on the roof, and got into the spirit of things by splashing a lot of paint very quickly and sloppily, on the rocks as well as on the building. Two young boys riding by on their bikes stopped to watch, and — shades of Tom Sawyer — happily joined the project when invited to do so. The dancer, unfortunately, slipped on a wet rock and twisted her back, but Summerlin continued to play until we were finished. Then everyone piled into the cars and returned to Rehoboth Beach.

That evening, several members of our group went to dine at a seafood restaurant. When they entered, they saw some of the old sailors who had been sitting on the dock that afternoon. The sailors recognized them, and there was a great deal of finger-pointing and merriment as they described that afternoon's scene to their dinner companions.

After the meal, we reassembled in our meeting room at the hotel and found that Gaudnek had set up a projector and was playing his videotapes of the afternoon, from both the harbor and the sea shanty. It was much funnier to us then than it had been in the afternoon, and we laughed at ourselves for most of an hour before getting down to business.

When Randolph convened the meeting that night, he introduced a newcomer to the group whose schedule had not permitted him to be there that afternoon. It was a young Pentecostal preacher and professor of homiletics from New York named James

Forbes — the same James Forbes who would later become senior minister of the prestigious Riverside Church.

"I have a question," said Forbes. "Just what does all of that stuff on the tapes have to do with salvation?"

I thought it was an excellent question. What *did* it have to do with salvation? But, as it happened, I was totally unprepared for the answer we heard. And so, I am sure, was Forbes. It came from a diminutive nun attached to the National Council of Churches office in New York, who was also visiting us for the first time. I regret that I don't remember her name.

"Don't you see?" said the little nun, her face aflame with passion. "Before we came, that was just an ordinary harbor, like every other harbor along the coast. Nothing unusual ever happened there. We made it come alive, simply by being there and doing what we did. You saw the faces of those men from the dock. And some of us saw them again at dinner tonight. They will never forget us and what we did. We transformed that harbor!

"The same is true of the little house by the sea," she continued. "It was a dying old shack when we arrived — dead, actually. It was rotting and falling apart. But we brought color and life and vibrancy to it, and to the rocks and the seaweed around it as well. Those little boys who joined us had a wonderful time. Like the sailors on the dock, they will never forget what they saw this afternoon, or that they took part in it.

"Don't you see?!" she exclaimed. "It *all* has to do with salvation!"

I'm not sure Forbes was persuaded. I have never asked him. But it was a magnificent speech, and the little nun was right. We *had* made a difference, an enormous difference.

And I realized, perhaps for the first time, what vastly divergent views people hold of salvation. Forbes saw it in a traditional way, as rescue, redemption, reclamation. He thought of it in terms of hearing about Jesus, repenting of sins, and accepting the kingdom of God. The nun, with all her vivacity, regarded it as awareness, perspective, sensitivity. She would have been happy talking religion with a Zen Buddhist.

Was one of them right and the other wrong? Were both right? One's answers to those questions would naturally depend on one's viewpoint. The thing is, the theology of salvation — what we sometimes call *soteriology*, from the Greek word *soteria* or "salvation" — is no longer a simple matter. In fact, the spectrum of opinions about it is extremely broad — much broader than most of us realize — and one's own place on that spectrum is probably the best key there is to one's position on a large number of other theological issues under discussion today.

I mention this episode as a prelude to a book that is about the changing nature of salvation from the time of the ancient Jews to our own day — or, more precisely, our changing perceptions of the nature of salvation.

We shall be talking about what the German theologians call *Heilsgeschichte,* the history or story of salvation. The only problem, as we now understand since Heisenberg, is that any subject under examination is affected by the one examining it. We cannot even walk through the scene of a crime without contaminating it. Our very approach to it compromises our conclusions.

So let us lay our cards on the table at the outset.

There are four basic premises to this book.

First, the so-called "biblical" view of salvation is itself a somewhat muddled concept. Actually, there are several biblical understandings of salvation, depending on which part of the Bible we read. Not only that, there was a jumble of ideas about salvation in the early Christian milieu, and it took at least three centuries to sort them out. And, even then, there is no guarantee that the general view that emerged was the "right" one, or that it prevailed over the other views for any sound and justifiable reason.

Second, nothing in this world, certainly no theological idea, is what it was a millennium ago. Nor even a century ago. Perhaps even a decade ago. Everything changes, evolves, mutates as the years pass. The rate of change is no longer linear, but exponential. Human intelligence itself is evolving at an incredible speed, largely because it has produced an artificial intelligence capable of augmenting what we know with an ever-increasing swiftness. We cannot even claim to think the way people thought a generation ago. Our very minds are being altered even as we read today's newspaper or answer today's e-mail. Perhaps — fair warning! — as we contemplate this subject.

Third — and derivatively — even the theological ideas of those who regard themselves as either liberal or conservative are vastly different from the liberal and conservative positions of earlier times. It is a simple fact that we cannot actually understand anything precisely as our forebears in earlier generations did. Conditions change, and, as they do, our thinking shifts, sometimes subtly, occasionally even dramatically. Many of us cling to the husks of ideas promulgated by religious groups dating back to the Reformation of the sixteenth century, but our understanding of those ideas is profoundly transformed by the lapse of time between then and now. Even the fundamentalists who profess to adhere to the doctrines of fundamentalism articulated in the late nineteenth and early twentieth centuries cannot begin to appreciate the world view that helped to shape their predecessors' opinions in a day when there were no automobiles, airplanes, or television sets and the only forms of electronic communication were the telegraph and the telephone.

And, fourth, there are probably more conceptions of the meaning of salvation today than we can begin to understand or document. In fact, there are as many ideas about personal salvation as there are persons in the modern world, even though many profess to adhere to views held by others in their faith communities. The British psychoanalyst R. D. Laing, in a book called *The Politics of Experience,* reminds us that no two persons can hold precisely the same viewpoint or understanding of anything. As we are all unique concatenations of atoms and experiences, he says, we must therefore possess singular impressions of the world and everything in it.

Almost every statement in this book, given what I have already said, must of necessity be either hyperbolic or inaccurate. It is literally impossible to say, "This is the exact view of salvation held by Roman Catholics at the end of the Middle Ages" or "Here is what the 'average' United Methodist churchgoer believes today." Such assertions hold validity only for the purpose of describing trends and currents within larger seas of ideas, not for capturing in precise detail what any particular individual actually believes.

Most individuals would in fact find it difficult, pushed to describe what they believe about salvation, to give an accurate and detailed description of their religious understanding. It is in our nature, having made our confessions of faith within the context of particular religious groups or families, to live our lives without giving very much thought to what we really believe, the way we continue, after a cursory introduction to kinetic anatomy, to run, jump, swim, sweep the floor, or swing at a golf ball without thinking about our bodies and how they function.

With this caution, then, let us begin our consideration of the meaning of salvation in our time by attempting a brief history of the term and what it has meant to men and women in the cultures that preceded ours.

One

Salvation in the Old Testament

It is hard for us in the contemporary world, with our moderately secure positions in comfortable surroundings and reliance on scientific health care, to imagine what was the most important thing in the mind of an individual in the ancient world, whether that individual lived in Israel, India, China, or the Americas. It was *survival.* That's right, sheer, plain survival — the ability to perdure, to continue existing, in an environment where everybody was constantly under threat by brigands, war, disease, and natural disasters.

The second most important thing was *success* — to have ample crops, an increase in one's lands and herds, a good marriage or marriages, the protection afforded by fortunate alliances, and the admiration, if not actual fear, of one's neighbors.

But in a world where existence itself was tenuous, where marauding bandits often laid waste to whole towns and mysterious diseases decimated the population of entire nations in a matter of days or weeks, it was survival, not success, that mattered most. Few people were ever notably successful, and being so was probably not regarded as a very attainable dream for the average person. Survival, on the other hand, was basic to everyone.

This is undoubtedly why the earliest version of salvation encountered in the Bible, or for that matter in any ancient literature, had to do with surviving and nothing else. There wasn't any real hope of a life beyond death when survival in this life had failed; everything was geared to a desperate need to maintain one's life in this world. That was clearly the bottom line.

Consider the case of Job, in the Old Testament book that most scholars believe is the oldest writing in the Hebrew scriptures.

Job is a morality tale about faithfulness to God, even in the maw of disaster, illness, and eventually death itself. The devil scoffs at the idea that there are men on earth who will worship God when their lives are seriously threatened, and he sets out to prove his case by arranging a series of staggering blows against God's servant Job.

Job's crops are destroyed, his herds stolen, his children killed, his very future wiped out. He himself is brought to the edge of death, his body covered by boils, so that he sits in the ashes all day and scrapes his festering flesh with a shard of pottery.

His wife, practical to a fault and undoubtedly anxious for his relief, counsels him to "curse God and die." But Job holds on, refusing to blame God for his misfortunes, and, according to the almost-too-facile end of the story, God rewards him for his faithfulness.

Job's situation raises some profound theological questions. Is he proud in his faith? Is that why God confronts him in a dreamlike sequence of events, showing him the wonders of creation and asking if he can really stand before the Creator of such miracles?

Must he be psychologically purged, after all he has been through, before God can compensate him for his faithfulness?

At any rate, God does reward Job's faithfulness by giving him a new family and new lands and bountiful crops, so that, as the text says, he had "twice as much as he had before" (Job. 42:10) and "the Lord blessed the latter days of Job more than his beginning" (Job 42:12).

There is no mention in the book that Job's "salvation" in any way involves an afterlife. The whole emphasis is on his survival, and, beyond that, on his success in the world. The book concludes on this note of satisfaction: "After this Job lived one hundred and forty years, and saw his children, and his children's children, four generations. And Job died, old and full of days" (Job 42:16–17).

The sum total of Job's salvation lay in his continued earthly existence and the way God recouped for him the things he had lost.

The Corporate Nature of the Soul

One of the concepts in Hebrew theology illustrated by the book of Job is that the *nephesh,* or soul, is not the highly individualized soul of Western culture but a network of interrelationships headed up or focused in the consciousness of a single person. Job's soul was "fat" at the beginning of his story, gorged with connections to children and possessions. It was reduced almost to nothing when all of these were removed, especially after he himself became ill and powerless. Then, when God had given him even more than he had before, it was enlarged and empowered again.

Johannes Pedersen, the great Semitic philologist, said in his classic study *Israel: Its Life and Culture* that the Hebrew language itself was much more collective and less specific than Greek or Latin. It "thought" in general terms, regarding individuals as part of an extended whole — a family, a tribe, a people — and not as distinctive selves, the way we think today.

We are so accustomed to regarding ourselves as separate persons, with no final connections to anyone except possibly through blood relationships, that it is almost impossible for us to imagine how an ancient Hebrew felt about his connection to the larger community. To him, salvation was something that belonged to the entire nation, not just to himself alone. When the Hebrews were in exile, they longed and prayed for the redemption of Israel. Then, and only then, would they ever be whole again.

The great soul, to the Hebrew mind, was one of force and power. It possessed strong life, and it was well-connected with others. The weak soul, on the other hand, was considered lonely and lifeless. If a man was out of favor with his friends and neighbors, he was cut off from the very source of his well-being and might as well be dead.

While Jesus never referred to this sense of communality directly, the implication was always there when he chided the Jews for being neglectful of the poor. The rich were never truly whole or healthy as long as they neglected those in poverty. This is part of the point of Jesus' story of the rich man and Lazarus (Luke 16:19–31). The rich man and his brothers thought themselves well off until the rich man died and, surprise, surprise, found himself in Hades. Looking up and seeing the poor man, Lazarus, who had sat at his gate day after day, hoping for a few crusts of bread or a bone with a little meat on it, now sitting at the side of Father Abraham, the man was astonished.

"Father Abraham," he called out, "have mercy on me, and send Lazarus to dip the tip of his finger in water and cool my tongue; for I am in agony in these flames." He recognized Lazarus, and felt some claim upon him, inasmuch as the man had so long dwelled outside his gate.

But the rich man had neglected his responsibility to Lazarus while they were alive, and so was deprived of his service after death. Abraham told him there was "a great chasm" fixed between them in the afterlife. Then, implored the rich man, fearful for the five brothers who had always been part of his soul's domain, send Lazarus to warn his brothers, so they might avoid coming to "this place of torment."

Again Abraham demurred. "They have Moses and the prophets," he said; "they should listen to them."

This is precisely the issue. The law and the prophets both stressed interpersonal responsibility for justice and welfare. But the wealthy often ignored their responsibility toward the poor and underprivileged. They accepted their solidarity with kinfolk and other well-to-do countrymen, but failed to recognize it with the neglected people Jesus sometimes called "my little ones."

When a man dies, the Hebrews believed, his soul goes from the world of sunlight and activity, where the strong and healthy live, to a world of darkness and inactivity, where all souls are powerless. This place of darkness and inactivity was called *Sheol.*

Sheol was often described as a common place of death to which all dead souls went, and each grave was considered a separate and isolated entrance to it. Pedersen called Sheol the "*Ur*-grave," the one in which all individual graves participate.[1] Each person who died was buried in his own, individual grave, but then became part of the general kingdom of death and was thought of as consorting with the dead.

The Finality of Sheol

There was not, in most of the writings of the Old Testament, any concept of life beyond death. People worshiped their gods as insurance, as a way of securing protection from disease, misfortune, and death. But when they died, they went to the dark, shadowy world of the dead, which was considered the deepest place in the universe, just as heaven, where God lived, was considered the highest. Souls who went to Sheol could never return. Many scriptural references suggest that it was a place of confinement where the gates were locked and bolted, so that no one, once there, could ever escape (Isaiah 38:10; Psalm 9:13; Job 17:16).

It is uncertain when the concept of Sheol, a shadowy underworld, began to develop, but it probably originated as an extension of people's experience of mind-racking pain or illness and also of the extreme discomfort and incapacity of old age. It appears to have been coextensive with the deeply troubled dreams and out-of-body experiences of the very elderly, a hallucinative state in which persons lost control over their normal functioning in life and became mere shadows of their former selves.

The Greek epic poems *The Iliad* and *The Odyssey* are filled with references to the shadowy underground called Hades, after the god of the underworld, where people are only phantasms of their former selves. Odysseus even makes a voyage there, across the

River Styx, and encounters the depressing landscape of a world
of death and perpetual dying. There was little if any comfort in
the thought of such a realm, for all who dwelled there appeared
to live in a state of morbidity and weakness.

Sheol, in the books of the Old Testament, was probably the
Hebrew version of Hades shared by most people in the Mediterranean region at that time. There is, for example, the passage in
1 Samuel 28, when Saul, confronted by the hosts of Philistines
gathered against him at Shunem, trembled for his safety. Praying,
he received no answer. So he asked his servants about a witch
or medium known to live at Endor, and, disguising himself and
accompanied by two servants, went to visit her at night.

"Consult a spirit for me," he directed her, "and bring up for me
the one whom I name to you" (1 Samuel 28:8).

The woman was afraid, and reminded him that the king, whom
she had not recognized, had ordered all mediums and wizards from
the land. He promised her immunity if she would obey him, and
she produced for him the spirit of the dead Samuel.

Saul could not see Samuel, but the woman reported what she
herself was seeing. It was an old man, a holy being, wrapped in
a robe.

Recognizing Samuel from her description, Saul fell to the
ground in obeisance.

Samuel asked why Saul had disturbed him by invoking his spirit.
Saul said he was desperate for assistance — that his armies were
outnumbered by the Philistines and in danger of being annihilated.

Samuel said that God was only doing to Saul what he, Samuel,
had been told he would do: he had taken away Saul's kingdom
and was giving it into the hands of David, his successor.

"Tomorrow," said the spirit, "you and your sons shall be with me" (1 Samuel 28:19).

There was no relief in these words for Saul. On the contrary, he fell to the ground and trembled with fear.

There was at the time no hope of an afterlife with God. Those who died were presumed to go to a shadowy realm where their spirits lingered in pitiable weakness and distress. If they continued to exist at all — a possibility encouraged by the vision of Samuel himself — it was in a hopeless condition, bereft of life and power.

What Saul wanted — his ultimate desire — was not an afterlife but continued existence in this life.

There are more than thirty references in the Old Testament to Sheol (often translated as "hell"), the place of the living dead.

The primary reference in the Torah is in Deuteronomy 32:22, where God, angry with the Israelites for their disobedience and their worship of strange gods, said that as they had made him jealous with gods that were not gods, he would provoke them with a people that were no people and would heap disasters upon them.

> For a fire is kindled by my anger,
> and burns to the depths of She'ol;
> it devours the earth and its increase,
> and sets on fire the foundations of the mountains.

Obviously, when Deuteronomy was written the concept of Sheol was common; else the reference would have been meaningless to those who read or heard it.

But there was no hint of belief in any semblance of a real afterlife to counterbalance it. When Moses gave the Ten Commandments to the children of Israel, they carried no promise of anything beyond well-being in this life, no suggestion that faithfulness to God would bring anything more than God's protection in this world.

As Jacob Neusner, a leading contemporary Hebrew scholar, says in *An Introduction to Judaism*, "Israel stood in a contractual relationship with God. God had revealed the Torah to Israel, and the Torah contained God's will for Israel. If Israel kept the Torah, God would bless the people, and if not — as Leviticus 26 and Deuteronomy 28 clearly explained — God would exact punishment for violation of the covenant."[2]

For centuries, Sheol was not even used as a threat against those who disobeyed God and the commandments. The formula was simply this: if the Israelites were faithful to God, they would enjoy long life and their blessings would pass to their children; if they were unfaithful, then they would die and their curse would be visited upon succeeding generations. Sheol didn't figure into it at all.

This was still the formula for the Sadducees, a religious party in the time of Jesus. The Pharisees, members of another religious group in the same era, had come, through intertestamental developments that were probably influenced by contact with non-Jewish religions, to believe in bodily resurrection. But the Sadducees did not believe in a real afterlife of any kind — only the weak and diminishing half-life of the grave — because they could find no warrant for it in the Torah, their sole guide to belief and practice.

By the time of the Book of Proverbs, though, parts of which were written as early as the tenth century BCE and others as late as the sixth century BCE, Sheol was beginning to be identified with divine punishment and retribution. There are several references to Sheol in this collection of wise sayings, and they are almost always in a context intended to encourage righteousness and discourage faithless or immoral behavior.

Those who abandoned the way of righteousness were known by God and would be punished because, just as God knew what was in Sheol, he knew the human heart (Proverbs 15:11). Parents were therefore admonished to discipline their children severely, beating them for the sake of their souls' salvation. "If you beat them with the rod, you will save their lives from She'ol" (Proverbs 23:14). Sheol and *Abaddon* (hell and destruction), the wise writer warned, are never satisfied (Proverbs 27:20), but are always hungry for more souls.

The combination of Sheol and Abaddon, used more than once in Proverbs, offers an interesting insight into the nature of Sheol. It was not a place of eternal punishment in the way succeeding generations came to imagine it, but it had become a general metaphor for death and despair, for ceasing to live in the world and dwelling in the midst of illness, cursedness, and evil.

The Evidence in the Psalms

The psalms were among the latest compositions included in the canon of the Hebrew scriptures. Therefore they may be expected to display the most recent theology of death and the afterlife. Yet they show very little development from this early concept of Sheol as a state or place of death and destruction.[3] Psalm 18:5, for example, purports to be a hymn of David composed to celebrate God's deliverance from his enemies:

> The cords of death encompassed me;
>> the torrents of perdition assailed me;
> the cords of She'ol entangled me;
>> the snares of death confronted me.

The psalm says that its composer called upon God for help, and God, hearing the cry from his temple, took action, sending his arrows against the psalmist's enemies and saving him.

There is a similar metaphor in the little book of Jonah, in the psalm supposedly composed by the prophet after God saved him from the belly of the great fish that had swallowed him:

> I called to the Lord out of my distress,
>> and he answered me;
> out of the belly of She'ol I cried,
>> and you heard my voice. (Jonah 2:2)

There is no suggestion here that Sheol was a place of eternal punishment. It was merely death itself, the nonexistence with which the prophet was threatened when he found himself in the depth of the waters with all the waves and billows passing over him.

Psalm 116, which is plainly a prayer of thanksgiving for recovery from illness, offers similar evidence. "The snares of death encompassed me," says the writer, "the pangs of She'ol laid hold on me; I suffered distress and anguish" (Psalm 116:3). Because

God heard the psalmist's cry and rescued him from his predicament, he professes to love the Lord, and promises: "therefore I shall call on him / as long as I live" (Psalm 116:2).

Note the words of this promise: the psalmist will call on God *as long as he lives.* There is no mention of praising God beyond death, for there is no expectancy of a life beyond death. In the Old Testament, it is life in this world that truly matters. There is no hope extended for anything beyond that.

Perhaps the nearest thing to an affirmation of life after death in the entire body of psalms comes in Psalm 139, the beautiful, lilting hymn to God's presence that declares:

> Where can I go from your spirit?
> Or where can I flee from your presence?
> If I ascend to heaven, you are there;
>   if I make my bed in She'ol,
> you are there. (Psalm 139:7–8)

The psalmist goes on to speak of how God has always known him, even from his mother's womb, and how important God's desires are to him. Doesn't he hate those who hate the Lord? Doesn't he count them as his enemies?

Then he concludes the psalm with these words:

> Search me, O God, and know my heart;
>   test me and know my thoughts.
> See if there is any wicked way in me,
>   and lead me in the way everlasting.
>   (Psalm 139:23–24)

Reading back from a more modern vantage point, we might be inclined to consider this reference to "the way everlasting" to be about eternal life. But that would be an inaccurate assumption, for the psalmist is merely praising God for a way of righteousness that is eternal, set forever in the heavens. He is not necessarily suggesting that his own life will be in any way everlasting.

Still, it is apparent that there was a general consciousness of a sort of three-layered universe, with heaven above, hell below, and earth in the middle, even though there was no expectation of the individual's being able to go to heaven. (The psalmist merely spoke of a supposition that he might travel up to heaven to find God.)

In the writings of Isaiah, the nation of Babylon is accused of having tried to establish itself in the heavens with God, only to be brought down to Sheol by his righteous power:

> You said in your heart,
>   "I will ascend to heaven;
> I will raise my throne
>   above the stars of God;
> I will sit on the mount of assembly
>   on the heights of Zaphon;
> I will ascend to the tops of the clouds,
>   I will make myself like the Most High."
> But you are brought down to She'ol,
>   in the depths of the Pit.
>   (Isaiah 14:13–15)

A number of references in the book of Ezekiel confirm that Sheol is only an equivalent of death and the grave. For example,

the enemies of God will be struck down and end up in Sheol along
with all the dead:

> For all of them are handed over to death,
>   to the world below;
> along with all mortals,
>   with those who go down to the Pit.
>   (Ezekiel 31:14b)

In the chapter following this, Ezekiel catalogues all those who
will be consigned to the Pit with the dead, a long list of the enemies of Israel that includes Egypt, Assyria, Elam, Edom, and
Sidonia. But still there is no suggestion that these peoples to be
slain by God will recognize each other in an infernal existence;
they will merely go down to death like all the other warrior nations
destroyed by the Lord.

The Book of Daniel

As H. H. Rowley has observed,[4] the singular instance of "a clear
and undisputed reference to the resurrection of the dead" in the
entire Old Testament occurs in the final chapter of the small
apocalyptic book of Daniel, written in the second century before
Christ, which pictures the Archangel Michael coming to the aid
of the Israelites: "At that time Michael, the great prince, the pro-
tector of your people, shall arise. There shall be a time of anguish,
such as has never occurred since nations first came into existence.
But at that time your people shall be delivered, everyone who is
found written in the book. Many of those who sleep in the dust of
the earth shall awake, some to everlasting life, and some to shame

and everlasting contempt. Those who are wise shall shine like the brightness of the sky, and those who lead many to righteousness, like the stars forever and ever" (Daniel 12:1–3).

Daniel was written at a time when Israel suffered extreme persecution at the hands of Antiochus IV of Syria, a fanatical Hellenist known as "Antiochus Epiphanes" because he declared himself Zeus and demanded to be recognized as a god. Eager to raise taxes to support his ongoing wars with the Egyptians, Antiochus scandalized the Jews by auctioning off the office of their high priest to the highest bidder. When the Jews revolted, he gave orders outlawing the Jewish religion and vigorously Hellenizing Jewish life.

Possessing a copy of the Torah, observing the Sabbath, and circumcising a child — the three basic symbols of Jewish observance — were all made punishable by death. And, to further exacerbate the situation, in 168 BCE Antiochus marched his troops into Jerusalem and erected an altar to Zeus in the temple, which was considered by all faithful Jews to be the ultimate sacrilege, or "an abomination of desolation."

Daniel, bearing the name of a well-known Jewish hero of the Ras Shamra literature, was part of a genre of protest writings designed to encourage the Jews in their belief that God would eventually vindicate his chosen people by destroying their enemies and restoring them to strength as a nation. Deliberately set in an earlier time, the Babylonian period, in order to make it appear as a prophecy, the book contains numerous historical errors. For example, Belshazzar, represented in chapter five as king of Babylon at the time of its destruction, was never actually a king, and Darius the Mede, appearing in chapter six as the conqueror of Babylon, did not even exist in that era, even though there were later monarchs of Persia named Darius.

Because of several things — a composite authorship, the predating and historical inaccuracies, and the fantastic or symbolical nature of many of the scenes and images in the book — Daniel is a dangerous minefield for interpreters. But it was readily seized upon by early Christians, as well as by exuberant and sometimes ill-informed Christians of every era since, as prophetic assurance that their understanding of salvation history would one day prevail. (In the Jewish canon, the book is placed among the Hagiographa, or "Sacred Writings," not among the writings of the prophets.)

Many scholars believe that Daniel's allusion to life after death is actually a sign of Persian, not Jewish, influence. But H. H. Rowley disagrees, preferring to think that "the author was driven by the dynamic of his own faith to this as the corollary of that faith."[5] Whatever the origin of the notion, this single bit of writing, questionable as it is among scholars, was to become the most important bridge between the general Old Testament idea of death-as-the-end-of-life and the New Testament understanding that death is only the gateway to judgment and an ongoing life on the other side of dying.

The Nature of Atonement

Because the religion of the early Hebrews had no defined notion of a real afterlife, but only a place of the dead roughly comparable to the shadowy realm of Hades in Greek mythology, the atonement of which their scriptures so often speak must be understood solely in terms of a negotiated arrangement with God that would extend people's lives and preserve them from human miseries of various kinds. It had nothing to do with life after death, as salvation would come to be associated with in the intertestamental period and time of the early Christians.

It was generally understood in the Old Testament world that every person sins, even those who don't intend to. In Solomon's prayer at the dedication of the temple he caused to be constructed, he says, "If they sin against you — for there is no one who does not sin..." (1 Kings 8:46). Therefore even good people were expected to offer sacrifices as an expiation for their sins and misdeeds. The whole system of sacrifice was built on this concept. God had given his people wisdom to resist sin and thus reduce its consequences — this was the constant theme of Proverbs and Sirach — but even then people sinned without knowing it, so their hearts needed cleansing and regeneration.

Over the years, a very intricate expiatory system was developed in Israel. Scholars discussed at length the nature of sacrifice and the kinds of offerings that would be effective for various kinds of offense. Jerusalem became of course the center of the sacrificial cultus — so completely that Jews often traveled there from distant parts of the world in order to offer sacrifices at the temple. This is why there was such grieving among the Jews over the years they spent in exile — they could not get to the temple to make the oblations that would improve their relationship to God. And it is why the loss of the temple, even though architecturally it was a building inferior to the king's palace, was so incredibly devastating to the Jews when it was destroyed. They had not merely lost a building, even the most holy, symbolic monument of their civilization, they had lost the center of their whole system of ritual atonement!

George Foot Moore, in his classic study *Judaism in the First Centuries of the Christian Era,* calls the general understanding among Jews that they could repent of their sins and offer sacrifices for them, thus invoking the total forgiveness of God, "the Jewish doctrine of salvation."[6] To every Jew from the time of Moses onward, this was the expectation, that if the sacrificial system was followed in all its prescriptions, both individually and collectively, they would be spared from divine wrath, given longer lives, and afforded more prosperous times.

An Understandable View of Salvation

Many of us who believe in an afterlife because of our religious faith or reports of those who have had life-after-life episodes in which they experienced life after death before being resuscitated probably consider the Old Testament view of salvation inadequate because it was concerned only with existence in this world. But anyone who has endured a near-fatal illness or injury, lived with a debilitating physical affliction such as multiple sclerosis, muscular dystrophy, Parkinson's disease, or Lou Gehrig's disease, or undergone severe chemotherapy, will understand the persuasiveness of a view of salvation that asks only for relief from pain and infirmity.

I myself underwent surgery on one of my lungs a few years ago, and in the process discovered what the promise of pain relief and extended life can mean. The surgery itself was not so bad, but a few days later my body released a shower of emboli into the affected area, making it nearly impossible for me to breathe. For days, I hovered between life and death, desiring to live only because I didn't want to leave my wife and family.

My life during those days was so marginal that it lacked almost all the quality of my normal existence. In the middle of the night, when my hospital room was quiet, I could feel myself hovering between this world and another, and I often thought what a relief it would be to die.

For months after this experience, I was still weak and unable to do many of the things I normally did. The blood thinner I was taking to protect me against further clotting made my capillaries so thin that the slightest blow or scrape brought great bruises or even open bleeding to my hands and arms. Often, I would awaken in the night and lie in the dark, thinking about my condition and how reduced it was from my usual robust way of living. I sometimes felt like a stranger in my own body, and wished I could return to the person I had once been.

It was during the early years of the war in Iraq, and I sympathized with all the soldiers and civilians who were being wounded in ways that would forever change their lives. Many returning service people had lost arms or legs or eyes, and they were having to adapt to a whole new manner of existence. Others were paralyzed, with no hope of ever recovering the use of their bodies.

Involuntarily, tears sprang to my eyes when I thought about these people and prayed for them. Most of them were half, a third, of my age and had long lives ahead of them.

Many of these unfortunate victims, I am sure, would have been happy at the time for a sense of physical salvation, believing that

God would heal them and give them a good life in this world, regardless of what might await them beyond death.

Reynolds Price's *A Whole New Life* is the famous writer's account of a four-year struggle to regain a semblance of his old life after doctors discovered a ten-inch tumor growing in his spinal cord. Suddenly a man who had enjoyed a happy, vigorous life found himself at the mercy of hospital attendants and nurses. The surgeon could excise only a portion of the tumor, and he chipped away bits of seven vertebrae to make more room for the remaining part.

In his first days in the hospital, Price could feel the numbness spreading down his legs, into his genitals, and throughout his lower body. A relative who spoke to the doctor was told this glum prognosis: "six months to paraplegia, six months to quadriplegia, six months to death."[7]

After weeks in the hospital, Price was taken home. The therapists had helped him to walk a little, so he wasn't completely helpless. But when he stood, he had to remain still for a few moments until he could reestablish some feeling in his legs and feet. Most of his lower body was numb. But there was a sharp, burning pain in his back, as if someone had laid a hot wire along the lower part of his spine. He often awoke in the night and felt the strangeness of his new existence.

Eventually fitted for a cast to keep him absolutely immobile, he was given numerous treatments of radiation therapy directed at the tumor. The radiologist who measured him for the cast told him there was a chance he could lose the use of both legs.

The night after he received this news, Price had a very meaningful dream. In it, he awoke from sleep in the early morning

beside the Sea of Galilee, which he had recently visited on a trip
to Israel. He recognized his surroundings, and he saw Jesus and
his disciples asleep in the grass nearby.

Then he saw the lean, tall figure of Jesus rise and come toward
him. Without speaking, Jesus motioned to him to follow. Quietly,
Price arose, took off his clothes without being bidden to do so,
and followed Jesus into the water of the lake. Silently, Jesus took
up handfuls of water and baptized him, letting the water run down
his body and across the puckered scar on his back.

"Your sins are forgiven," said Jesus. It was the only thing he
said. Then he turned and started out of the lake.

Price followed him. It wasn't his sins he was worried about.
"Am I also cured?" he wanted to know.

"That too," said Jesus, without looking back, and continued on
his way.

"I followed him out," says Price, "and then, with no palpable
seam in the texture of time or place, I was home again in my wide
bed."[8]

Price is a Christian, even though he confesses it is in "an un-
churchly Christianity which was passed to me by my parents."[9]
But his concern, throughout his ordeal of radiation and recovery — the radiation was horrible, like "going to Hiroshima every
day for lunch" — was not for the vaunted Christian dream of life
after death. It was for peace, for energy, for the ability to live in
reasonable comfort and strength each day.

At one point, when he was living with a cousin, he told her
about his dream of being anointed by Jesus. Remembering that
in his childhood he had spent a lot of time drawing, she asked

him to sketch what he had experienced. Taking pen and paper, he drew in the essential lines of Jesus cupping his hand with the water and letting it flow over him. Strangely, he said, it gave him momentary relief from the burning pain in his back.

Over the next two years, he made dozens of similar drawings. Each one, he says, became a meditation on the face of Jesus — the face that has "driven Western art for more than a thousand years." He was fascinated by Jesus, and by his relationship to him.

Yet he was not seeking eternal life. He was after healing. He wanted wholeness in this life.

"I know that the drawings became my main new means of prayer," says Price, "when my earlier means were near exhaustion. By now I'd asked a thousand times for healing, for ease and a longer life. But calamity proceeded, and even the repetition of 'Your will be done' had come to sound empty. So the drawings were a sudden better way, an outcry and an offering. If they asked for anything, I suppose it was what I still ask for daily — for life as long as I have work to do, and work as long as I have life."[10]

I reread *A Whole New Life* after my own experience in the hospital and understood it more completely than I had the first time. When people are hurting, when their bodies, which have always served them faithfully and responsively, cease to be dependable, it isn't life after death they really care about. It is a restoration to wholeness and power in this life, a recovery of the ease and carefreeness with which they once functioned in their everyday existence.

I thought about Job and how he must have felt in those dark days when he had buried his children, his body was wracked by pain and disease, and he had lost his lands and cattle. At that point, Job wasn't concerned about life after death. He wanted to feel all right again, to climb out of the pit where his soul was writhing in torment, to experience the joy and satisfaction he had once found in life. A view of salvation that focused on being okay in this life was enough for Job; in fact, it was all that he could imagine.

Two

Salvation in
the New Testament

It is apparent, from certain things said in the Gospels, that the concept of salvation among the Jews had undergone some very profound changes between the closing of the Hebrew scriptures and the time of the New Testament. All three synoptic Gospels (Matthew, Mark, and Luke), for example, carried the story of Jesus' encounter with a group of Sadducees, an elite religious party that rejected belief in an afterlife because it is not mentioned in the Torah, the only doctrinal source they accepted (Matthew 22:23–33; Mark 12:18–27; Luke 20:27–40).

Some of the Sadducees, "who say there is no resurrection," came to Jesus with a question designed to trap him. Moses, they pointed out, had commanded that if a married man died childless, his brother should marry his wife and raise up children on behalf of his deceased sibling. Suppose, they taunted, there were seven brothers. The first to marry died, leaving no offspring, so the second married the widow. He also died with no progeny. The third then married her, and so on, until she had been married to all

seven brothers. When the seventh had died, and she also, whose
wife would she be in heaven?

Jesus' answer was twofold: First, those who die and go to heaven
are like the angels, and are not troubled by marital structures.
Second, if the Sadducees had been as ardent in their scriptural
studies as they claimed to be, they would have noticed that God
told Moses at the burning bush, "I am the God of Abraham, the
God of Isaac, and the God of Jacob," not "I *was* their God." Therefore the patriarchs are still living in an afterlife with God, though
they died centuries ago.

It may be inferred from the Gospels, and is confirmed by the
first-century Jewish historian Josephus, that the Pharisees, the
most influential religious group in Palestine at the time of Jesus,
believed that the soul survives death and is rewarded or punished
in another life for its deeds in this one. As no rabbinic literature
survives from that era, we have no way of knowing more than this.
It is impossible to say whence the Pharisees derived a belief in the
afterlife, but it may well have filtered into Jewish theology through
the mystery religions that were so widespread in the Greco-Roman
world, or, conceivably, it came from the book of Daniel and its
introduction of the idea that God would redeem his people from
death and make them shine like stars in the firmament.

The so-called mystery religions were rife in the Mediterranean
area from a century before Christ until two or three centuries after
his death. They were all built around "secret" personalities, ideas,
and rituals, and the people inducted into them swore to preserve
the secrets — hence the term "mystery" religions. There were
mystery cults formed around the mythical characters Dionysus,
Mithra, Cybele, Adonis, and dozens of others. Both Adonis and

Osiris were said to have died and returned to life. In the cult of Dionysus, followers are known to have slain bulls over an open pit, reveled in their blood — even drinking it — and celebrated Dionysus's dismemberment and being resurrected to new life.

Many scholars, such as Joscelyn Godwin and Maarten Vermaseren, have claimed to see relationships between such mystery cults and the early Christians, particularly in the emphasis on Christ's blood and the resurrection. It is impossible to say with any certainty whether this relationship actually existed. But there can be little doubt that the widespread existence of the mystery cults helped to popularize the notion of life after death, and may well have influenced the Pharisees' belief in an afterlife.

When Christianity was born in Palestine and surrounding countries, the notions of resurrection and an afterlife were quite common, and the religion of Jesus spread rapidly among a populace eager to embrace a new cultic figure who was reported to have risen from the dead after being crucified by the resented Roman government.

Salvation in the Gospels

We seldom think of salvation as an evolving concept. Yet it is obvious, if we reflect on it, that even in early Christianity there was more than one viewpoint about what it meant to be saved.

First, there was the enduring concept of salvation as something God would give to the Jews. This is why there was so much emphasis on Jesus as the Messiah, the Savior sent from God to redeem his people, Israel. This element runs through the Gospels, and it receives final confirmation when Jesus weeps over the city of Jerusalem because it has not truly received him as the Savior appointed by God.

Second, there was the notion of salvation as personal forgiveness, as in the case of the paralytic man lowered into Jesus' presence through a hole in the roof (Mark 2:1–12). When Jesus saw the faith of the men who carried their friend to the roof and lowered him, he said to the paralyzed man, "Son, your sins are forgiven." Thus Jesus related salvation or redemption to its classical meaning in Israel, as atonement and reconciliation with God.

Third, there was the idea of salvation as personal wholeness or wellness. When blind Bartimaeus was brought to Jesus, Jesus asked him, "What do you want me to do for you?" Bartimaeus said, "My teacher, let me see again." Jesus replied, "Go; your faith has made you well" (Mark 10:46–52). Jesus frequently "saved" people by casting demons out of them and restoring them to normal life, as in the case of the Gadarene demoniac (Mark 5:1–20) and the boy who was dashed to the ground by a spirit (Mark 9:14–29).

Fourth, there was also the concept of salvation as wholeness in one's family or restoration to community, as in the case of Zacchaeus, the tax collector (Luke 19:1–10). When Jesus called Zacchaeus down from the tree where he had climbed in order to see the Messiah and went home with him, Zacchaeus was so moved that he gave half of his goods to the poor and swore to repay with interest anyone he had wronged in his office as a tax collector. Jesus' response was: "Today salvation has come to this house, because he too is a son of Abraham. For the Son of Man came to seek out and to save the lost."

Fifth, by the time the Gospel of John was written, the idea of salvation from sin with the reward of eternal life had become an important theme. Jesus announces to Nicodemus, a leader of the Jews, that "whoever believes in him [i.e., Jesus] may have eternal life" (John 3:15), and declares a second time that "everyone who believes in him may not perish but may have eternal life" (John 3:16). When a crowd follows him for food, he chastises them, "Do not work for the food that perishes, but for the food that endures for eternal life, which the Son of Man will give you" (John 6:27). When he raises Lazarus from the dead, he declares, "I am the resurrection and the life. Those who believe in me, even though they die, will live, and everyone who lives and believes in me will never die" (John 11:25–26a).

Ralph G. Wilburn, in his carefully reasoned work *The Historical Shape of Faith,* sees three distinct views of history, and therefore of salvation, in the New Testament as a whole. Paul and most early Christians, including Ignatius, Polycarp, Barnabas, and Irenaeus, shared the notion of an imminent return of Christ that would bring all history to an end and establish the kingdom of God on earth. The letter to the Hebrews and the book of Revelation reveal another understanding, that Christ's return may not be as soon as was generally expected; so they offer a "futuristic eschatology," encouraging believers to cling to their faith in spite of an interim period of indeterminate length. The Gospel of John, one of the latest books in the New Testament canon, displays yet a third view, that of a "radical contemporizing of eschatology" — the notion, called "realized eschatology" by Rudolf Bultmann, the famous New Testament scholar at the University of Marburg, that Jesus' second coming occurred with the bestowal of his spirit.[11]

Even the most cursory study of the four Gospels reveals an obvious progression in soteriological thought from the synoptics — which viewed Jesus in the traditional role as the Messiah of Israel who healed people, called them to repentance, and condemned those who rejected his appeal — to the Fourth Gospel, in which the predominant emphasis is on Jesus as the Son of the Father, indeed, *one with the Father,* who summons individuals to believe in him and receive eternal life. The invitation to eternal life is issued again and again in the Fourth Gospel, and divine judgment (the Greek *krisis*) is implicit in the response individuals, the Jews, and the world as a whole made to it.

What all of this means is that Christians during the first two or three centuries held very varied and fluid interpretations of Jesus' messiahship. They were vigorously thrashing out the meaning of his coming for their salvation. And, in the process, they moved from traditional messianism, the Jewish understanding that God would save the nation of Israel, to a highly personal concept of redemption that conformed more agreeably to a Hellenistic notion of religion, in which it was the salvation of the individual, not the race or national grouping, that was deemed most important.

The Pauline Concept of Salvation

The one person who did the most to shape the early Christian church's theology was the Apostle Paul, whose story of a radical conversion from Judaism, in which he actually persecuted Christians, to ardent discipleship for Jesus of Nazareth, is narrated in the Acts of the Apostles (9:1–22). Paul claimed to have met the risen Christ on the road to Damascus, an encounter that left him physically blind until God sent a man named Ananias to touch his eyes and restore his sight. At once, after his sight was returned, Paul began traveling among the synagogues of Asia Minor, announcing to all the Jews that Jesus was the Son of God. Some Christians were suspicious and afraid of him, and many Jews sought to kill him as a blasphemer. But eventually he won acceptance from the Christians in Jerusalem and was ordained to preach to the Gentiles.

Even though he was sent to the Gentiles — some speculate that this was to get him out of the hair of Peter and the other Christians in Jerusalem — he continued to enter synagogues wherever he went and to use them as a base from which to declare the gospel among the population in general.

What was Paul's message of salvation? The answer is recorded succinctly in Acts 16:25–34, the story of Paul and Silas's imprisonment in Philippi, a Roman city. At midnight, while the missionaries were praying and singing hymns, an earthquake shook the city, opening the prison's doors. The jailer, jostled out of bed to find his prison in ruins, was astonished to find that the two prisoners had not fled. Bringing them out of their cell, he asked, "Sirs, what must I do to be saved?"

It would be the sinner's classic question to God's heralds. Paul and Silas answered, "Believe on the Lord Jesus, and you will be saved, you and your household." That would become the stock phrase for Christian evangelists through the centuries.

When I was a young man entering the ministry, at the age of seventeen, I came upon a small, pocket-sized tract by a Murfreesboro, Tennessee, preacher named John R. Rice, featuring a drawing of an open prison door on its cover, plus the bold title, "What Must I Do to Be Saved?" Within the pamphlet, the preacher described what it meant to believe on the Lord Jesus, confess him before others, and find God's eternal salvation.

I was away at college, and I sent my father a tie for his birthday. Because my father was not a Christian, I slipped one of these tracts into the box with the tie. My father never mentioned it to me, but I felt, at the time, that I had witnessed with the most effective means I had. The little story of Paul and Silas in the Philippian prison was a capsule version of the meaning of salvation.

Paul's theology of Christ, or Christology, was probably stated most clearly in his letter to the Philippian Christians in the hymn or poem known as a "kenotic" psalm, from a Greek word meaning to "empty" oneself:

> Let the same mind be in you that was in Christ Jesus,
>   who, though he was in the form of God,
>   did not regard equality with God
>   as something to be exploited,
>   but emptied himself,
>   taking the form of a slave,
>   being born in human likeness.
> And being found in human form,
>   he humbled himself
>   and became obedient to the point of death —
>   even death on a cross.
>
> Therefore God also highly exalted him
>   and gave him the name
>   that is above every name,

so that at the name of Jesus
every knee should bend,
　　in heaven and on earth and under the earth,
and every tongue should confess
　　that Jesus Christ is Lord,
　　to the glory of God the Father.

　　　　　　　　　　　　　　　　　(Philippians 2:5–11)

The words may not originally have been Paul's — he sometimes appropriated the church's new hymnody without crediting authors — but they express his adoration for Christ as a preexistent being in the same way that the prologue to the Fourth Gospel does when it declares, speaking of Christ as the Word or prime ordering principle of everything, that "In the beginning was the Word, and the Word was with God, and the Word was God" (John 1:1).

Apparently Paul never knew Jesus in the flesh, during his years as an itinerant rabbi in Palestine, but had one unforgettable encounter with him in his resurrected form on the road to Damascus. This might at least partially explain why Paul always identified Christ as an eternal being, exalted and triumphant in heavenly power.

For Paul, salvation meant literally being in Christ. Martin Dibelius, the German scholar, spoke in *Paul* of the Apostle's "Christ mysticism" because of his fondness for the phrase *"en christo"* in his many writings. Paul's entire posture, as a convert and an apostle, was "in Christ," as if his only way of viewing the world, once he had met the risen Savior, was through Christ's eyes and purposes. Being in Christ determined his life's work, his moral stance, his regard for others, his way of looking at absolutely everything.

As Dibelius points out, Paul didn't have the words "Christian" or "Christianity" yet, so he had to improvise to speak of what it meant for people to be Christian. It was therefore natural to speak of himself or others as being "in Christ" as a way of expressing their new state.[12]

Paul was in prison when he addressed a letter to his Christian friends at Philippi. Yet he wrote:

> I will continue to rejoice, for I know that through your prayers and the help of the Spirit of Jesus Christ this will turn out for my deliverance. It is my eager expectation and hope that I will not be put to shame in any way, but that by my speaking with all boldness, Christ will be exalted now as always in my body, whether by life or by death. For to me, living is Christ and dying is gain. (Philippians 1:18b–21)

It would be hard to imagine a more dynamic servant of an idea or a relationship. Here was a man who was one of the world's great geniuses, devoted to the cause of a man who had died on a cross as an enemy of the Roman state, and he appears never to have flagged in his energy or enthusiasm. It was he, more than any other human being, who popularized Christianity in the world at large and contributed to the conception of human redemption as depending solely on each individual's response to the overtures of God in Christ.

Perhaps the secret of Paul's success as a witness to Christ was the way he cunningly (and sometimes even unwittingly) managed to syncretize various strands of Hellenistic thought to produce a triumphant version of his own faith. Like the Gnostics, he was willing to posit a good world and an evil world, one transcendent and the other immanent. For Paul, the world we live in is the world of the flesh, and the flesh is always inferior to the soul or spirit. He believed the only way we could be saved from this sordid existence is by God's reaching in from his transcendent realm and making our salvation possible. This he did in Christ. And, as in the various mystery religions, we appropriate this salvation in Christ through our faith and the expression of cultic acts, in our case baptism and the Lord's Supper.[13]

In the letter to the Romans, his magnum opus, Paul lays out the basics of his theology: All humanity is guilty, and falls short of the glory of God. We are all therefore deserving of eternal punishment. The vaunted law of the Jews is no excuse, as no one is capable of keeping it in its entirety. The only righteousness that really matters is the righteousness of God, which he has shown willingness to impute to those who have faith in him. Even Abraham, the acknowledged father of the Jews, was made righteous through faith and not through works. Jesus' death on the cross was God's final, climactic statement of God about human inadequacy and divine forgiveness. By accepting Jesus, we receive atonement for our sins and have peace with God. Thereafter, sin has no dominion over us; we are free to live and walk in the Spirit of God. Those who live in the Spirit will be raised up after death to live forever with Christ. We need not, therefore, fear death or punishment; our hope is in God, regardless of what the world does to discourage us.

Paul wishes, he says, that God would save the Jews. But they too must recognize the action that God has taken in Christ. It is clear what we must do in order to be saved: "If you confess with your lips that Jesus is Lord and believe in your heart that God raised him from the dead, you will be saved" (Romans 10:9). There is no difference between Jews and Greeks. "The same Lord is Lord of all and is generous to all who call on him. For, 'Everyone who calls on the name of the Lord shall be saved'" (Romans 10:12–13). He says the Jews still have a chance to be saved, if they will only hear the word of the Lord.

Yet he sees a positive, upbeat side to the Jews' blindness and stumbling about, and that is that it allowed the gospel of Christ to cross Israel's borders to the Gentiles. And when the "full number" of Gentiles has come into the kingdom, then the Jews will be saved, as God promised, because "the gifts and the calling of God are irrevocable" (Romans 11:20). God has shown mercy to the Gentiles by permitting them to enter the kingdom, and later he will show mercy to his chosen people as well. "O the depth of the riches and wisdom and knowledge of God! How unsearchable are his judgments and how inscrutable his ways!" (Romans 11:33)

Now, because we have received new life in Christ Jesus, Paul declares that it is important to present ourselves to God as living sacrifices, holy and acceptable, and to have our very beings transformed from worldly concerns to those of the Spirit. We should live in accord with one another, realizing that we have different gifts, and we should share in the ministry of Christ. We should genuinely love one another, hate evil, and hold fast to whatever is good. We should never seek vengeance on our enemies, but should feed them when they are hungry and give them drink when they are thirsty, thus overcoming evil with good. We should live peaceably under the civil authorities and care for those who are weak in the faith. Religious practices are not important in and of themselves, but may be important to some people, so we should respect them. And we should live with alertness, heading off those who would cause dissensions and offenses in the fellowship, because God will soon crush Satan under our feet.

Paul's letter is unarguably the greatest mandate of salvation that Christians possess. It provides the rationale for salvation (all have sinned and are in need of it), the means of salvation (Christ died for our sins), the appeal of salvation (it is a free gift from God for those who will accept it), the results of salvation (God puts his Spirit within us to live transformed and transforming lives), the rules of salvation (we are to live in love, humility, and hope), and the final outcome of salvation (God will crush the Evil One and redeem the saved). More than any other piece of Christian literature, even the Gospels, this one spells out the plan and magnitude of Christ's saving power for the believer, and, more than any other writing, it would become the model for evangelical understanding through the centuries.

Was Paul influenced by the mystery religions so widespread in his culture? This question has been the topic of many books and articles, and the answer is that no one can know for sure. The structure of his soteriology does reflect the kind of passion and wholeness one finds in what we know of the mystery cults. They too insisted that participants in their rites and beliefs have their beings consumed by the deities they worshiped. By coming together in secret and observing the rituals of their cultic groups, they became empowered by their deities to live transcendent existences and not be overcome by problems and difficulties.

Outwardly, nothing changed in their lives; inwardly everything was different.

Perhaps the answer, if we could know it, would not be of any great consequence. Paul must have known something about the plethora of mystery groups swarming about him in the empire, especially during his years in Tarsus, which was a mecca for eso-teric religions. But it may have been a case of the culture's having provided him with a psychological framework for receiving and transmitting the gospel of Christ in a way that ensured its sur-vival and, not only that, its eventual dominance in the culture of the Western and Middle Eastern worlds.

The gospel we received from Paul is, to be sure, a changed and expanded version of the one we find in the Gospels themselves, especially the synoptics. He has left it indelibly impressed with his own theology and that of unknown Christians in his era who might have influenced him to think as he did. But, as I have already said, every person holds a view of salvation that is at least partially unique to him- or herself, and our understanding of the meaning of salvation is always in flux according to personal and cultural factors that have a bearing on it. There is no such thing as a "pure" understanding of salvation, and Paul was simply bolder in expressing his brilliant interpretation of it than any other follower of Jesus.

Hebrews and Revelation

The letter to the Hebrews, accepted as the work of Paul until modern times when textual studies became more advanced and it was determined to be the product of an anonymous author, added little to the doctrine of salvation he expounded. But, purporting to be a message of encouragement to Jewish Christians around the world of that time, it did accomplish two things related to the doctrine. First, it underlined the relationship between Jesus' sacrifice on the cross and the sacrificial system of Jewish history. And second, it further endorsed the idea of individual atonement, even for Jews, over the notion of national salvation that had once been Israel's ideal.

Paul had often spoken about Jesus' death as a sacrifice offered for the sins of the people (as did the Gospel of John), but the author of Hebrews made this a central theme of his letter. He was obviously mindful of how deeply ingrained in Jewish consciousness was the habit of offering sacrifices for sins, both personal and corporate, and how important the temple in Jerusalem was to Jews living all over the Mediterranean area. So when he introduced the image of Jesus as "a great high priest who has passed through the heavens" (Hebrews 4:14), he must have realized that he had hit on a subject that must be exploited much more fully.

Every high priest the Jews have known, he says, has been chosen by mortals and has served God by offering sacrifices for the sins of "the ignorant and wayward." But, as the priest is himself subject to sin, he must also offer sacrifices for himself. Jesus, on the other hand, was appointed not by mortals but by God. "You are my Son," said God; "today I have begotten you." God also said, "You are a priest forever, according to the order of Melchizedek" (Hebrews 5:5–6). In his mortal life, Jesus learned submission to his heavenly Father through his own sufferings. But unlike other priests, he did not himself sin; instead, he went on to perfection and "became the source of eternal salvation for all who obey him" (Hebrews 5:9).

In good Hellenistic fashion, the author of Hebrews declares that ordinary priests "offer worship in a sanctuary that is a sketch and shadow of the heavenly one" (Hebrews 8:5). But Jesus, who has died as the supreme and everlasting sacrifice, now makes intercession for his people in the heavenly sanctuary. "He entered once for all into the Holy Place, not with the blood of goats and calves, but with his own blood, thus obtaining eternal redemption" (Hebrews 9:12). Thus he is now the mediator of a new and eternal covenant between God and his people. The old covenant wasn't invalid; it was merely superseded by a greater one. The law was only "a shadow of the good things to come" for God's people. Now, as Christ has offered the great sacrifice for all time, canceling the need for others, he has sanctified his people for eternity.

Having thus connected the religion of Jesus with the religion of the old Israel, the writer then proceeds to outline what it means to have a life of faith in Christ. He knows he is writing to people who are suffering persecution, as well as to others who cannot understand why the kingdom of God had not arrived with the coming of the Messiah, so he wants to emphasize the importance of individual fidelity to the Lord. "Faith," he says, "is the assurance of things hoped for, the conviction of things not seen" (Hebrews 11:1).

He deftly illustrates this statement by appealing to the examples of great Jewish icons, going all the way back to Abel, the son of Adam. The catalogue would include Enoch, Noah, Abraham, Isaac, Jacob, Moses, Rahab, Gideon, Barak, Samson, Jephthah, David, Samuel, and the prophets, as well as all the saints who had more recently remained faithful to God in spite of being mocked, flogged, cast into prison, and put to death. They have all, he says, "died in faith without having received the promises" (Hebrews 11:13a).

"Therefore," he concludes in his magnificent peroration, which has been repeated by countless preachers through the centuries, "since we are surrounded by so great a cloud of witnesses, let us also lay aside every weight and the sin that clings so closely, and let us run with perseverance the race that is set before us, looking to Jesus the pioneer and perfecter of our faith, who for the sake of the joy that was set before him endured the cross, disregarding its shame, and has taken his seat at the right hand of the throne of God" (Hebrews 12:1–2).

It was a marvelous appeal!

The book of Revelation, or the Apocalypse, likewise added little to the picture of salvation sketched by Paul, but its cartoon-like cosmic drama has always had a great attraction for Christians, from the illiterate peasants of the Middle Ages to the millions of readers of the *Left Behind* books in our own time. It begins simply enough, with a promise to show God's servants "what soon must take place," then it moves immediately into a description of "the seven churches that are in Asia," probably caricatures of churches that actually existed but dramatized to preach lessons about faithfulness and righteousness during a time of trial for confessing Christians.

Next it shows the Lamb of God, the apocalyptic figure of the Son, being hymned by "every creature in heaven and on earth and under the earth and in the sea" and opening seven great seals to reveal things that would come to pass. One displayed a white horse and a conquering rider. Another showed a black horse whose rider carried a pair of scales. Yet another revealed all the souls that had been slaughtered for the faith, crying out, "Sovereign Lord, holy and true, how long will it be before you judge and avenge our blood on the inhabitants of the earth?" (Revelation 6:10).

Finally, John attests to seeing an angel descending from the risen sun, bearing the great seal of God and crying out to the four angels in charge of the earth to withhold their terrible punishment until all the saints of the Lord have been marked with God's sign on their foreheads. First, he says, he heard the number of all the saints from the tribes of the Hebrews, twelve thousand from each; then he looked and saw "a great multitude that no one could count, from every nation, from all tribes and peoples and languages, standing before the throne and before the Lamb, robed in white, with palm branches in their hands. They cried out in a loud voice, saying,

> 'Salvation belongs to our God who is
> seated on the throne, and to the
> Lamb!'" (Revelation 7:9–10)

Images like this must have held great inspiration for Christians in an era of persecution, whether they were Jews or Gentiles, for they were grand, sweeping, and at times even militaristic, suggesting that believers were part of the universal drama of the ages and that God was preparing to wreak vengeance on the earth for all their suffering. Such depictions are well known to have been comforting and encouraging for African Americans during their time of slavery, and they have always been the special province of preachers addressing crowds of underprivileged persons, such as the poor in Africa, Asia, and Central and South America who have flocked to Pentecostalism.

After another series of heart-lifting glimpses of God's vengeance against the wicked and unfaithful, and hearing about the fall of Babylon, the great whore of a city that stands for all the evil powers of the earth, John describes the binding of Satan, the mighty serpent, and his being thrown in a pit for a thousand years. During this millennial interim, the souls of those who were beheaded for accepting and preaching the gospel come to life and reign with Christ.

At the end of the thousand years, Satan is released from prison for one last try at dominating the earth. He goes through the nations, lying and deceiving people in order to draft them for battle. They march up and down on the earth, and surround the camp of the saints and the beloved city of God. This time, fire rains down from heaven and consumes all of them, and the devil is thrown into a lake of fire and sulfur, where he will be tormented day and night forever and ever.

Then John says he saw the great white throne of God, and the One who sat on it. All the dead, both great and small, stood around the throne, while the book of life was opened. Everybody, even the souls that had been in Hades, was judged according to the good or evil he had done in his life. Anyone whose name was not found in the book of life was thrown into the lake of fire with the devil.

Finally, John describes the new heaven and new earth he beheld, and the holy city, the new Jerusalem, coming down out of heaven "prepared as a bride adorned for her husband" (Revelation 21:2). He heard a loud voice from the throne saying,

"See, the home of God is among mortals.
He will dwell with them as their God;
they will be his peoples,
and God himself will be with them;
he will wipe every tear from their eyes.
Death will be no more;
mourning and crying and pain will be no more,
for the first things have passed away."

(Revelation 21:3–4)

It is a masterful picture of the way everything is supposed to turn out for believers. Their salvation will be complete. They not only will be rescued from sadness, distress, and disease, but will be led triumphant over death itself, to reign with Christ in heaven forever and ever. Cartoonish it may be. But it is also deeply stirring and affecting to those who believe and accept the gospel as an accurate measure of the way life in the universe will turn out.

As one pastor told me after reading several of the *Left Behind* books, "I know it is a simplistic portrait of the way everything is supposed to end. But I can't help finding it strangely moving. It speaks to me in this nightmare of a world and enables me to sleep at night."

The Importance of Conversion

"Believe on the Lord Jesus Christ, and you will be saved" (Acts 16:31). In all the New Testament, this is the understanding about salvation. From the earliest texts (some of Paul's letters and the Gospel of Mark) to the latest (the Gospel of John), a period of some three-quarters of a century, it is the word that covers them all. If Jesus was first understood as the human being anointed as God's Messiah, according to the promises to Israel, and came in a short time to be regarded as the preexistent Christ who had come not just to save the Jews but to liberate the whole world, it was an understandable leap.

There was never, as we shall see in the next chapter, a complete unanimity of understanding about Christ's person and his work. But there was, at the heart of every personal soteriology, an acceptance of the witness placed in the mouths of Paul and Silas in that Philippian jail: that, whatever constituted salvation — whether it was restoration of the body from a withered arm or a debilitating illness, or rescue from occupying powers, either real or demonic, or the granting of life after death — its only condition was belief in the Lord Jesus Christ.

One of the New Testament's main themes, then, along with the insistence on belief in Jesus as the Christ, was the matter of conversion. The Greek word for it was *metanoia,* or the transforming of the mind. This is why Paul began his hymn to the self-emptying Christ in Philippians 2 with the words "Let this mind be in you." As Gentiles came to a gospel born in the land of the Jews, and as Jews themselves were urged to accept a Messiah unlike any they had expected, being converted was the sine qua non of a new relationship with God.

Apparently there was almost a fever of conversion among those who heard the gospel from its first preachers. At Pentecost alone, three thousand male visitors to Jerusalem, along with whatever families may have accompanied them, made the switch to Jesus. Wherever Paul and the other apostles went, they preached for conversions. The early church, by the very nature of its situation, was a gathering of converts.

Later, when the church had become established, it would be different. But in the Reformation of the fifteen hundreds, after long centuries of relative indifference to whether a person was actually converted or born of the Spirit, conversion would once again become a battle cry, and it would remain so for evangelicals until this day. They have always believed, as the famous evangelist Billy Sunday declaimed, that going to church doesn't make one a Christian any more than sitting in the garage makes one an automobile!

Christian history is full of the stories of famous converts, beginning with Paul himself on the Damascus Road. Augustine (354–430) was converted from a life of libertinism to become the greatest theologian of the Middle Ages. He tells in his *Confessions* how he was sitting in a garden, weeping over his sins, when he heard a child's voice saying, "Pick it up, read it; pick it up, read it." Taking up the Bible and reading the first verse upon which his eyes naturally fell, he saw this admonition: "Not in rioting and drunkenness, not in chambering and wantonness, not in strife and envying, but put on the Lord Jesus Christ, and make no provision for the flesh to fulfill the lusts thereof" (Romans 13:13). His decision was instantaneous: he would spend his life living for Christ!

Blaise Pascal (1623–1662), the influential scientist, theologian, and author, had a similarly dramatic conversion, in the form of a vision that came to him when he was thirty-one, and it demanded the rest of his life. He wrote the essence of it down in something he called "The Memorial," sewed it into the lining of his jacket, and left it there, where it was found after his death ten years later. The most prominently inscribed word, in capital letters, was "FIRE." Apart from that, the memento is almost an incoherent babbling of phrases of praise and confession, with the fervent prayer, "Let me never be separated from him."

C. S. Lewis (1898–1963), one of the most famous Christian apologists in the world, told in *Surprised by Joy* how God "closed in" on him as he was riding on the top of a double-decker bus going up Headington Hill in Oxford, where he was a tutor at the university. He said that he became aware that he was holding something at bay, or shutting it out of his life. He had the sensation of being enclosed in very stiff clothing, or even in armor. Suddenly he realized that he had "a free choice." He could either remain inside the armor or he could burst out and be a new man. He "chose" to unbuckle the armor and emerge. For many nights after that, alone in his room at Magdalen College, he felt "the steady, unrelenting approach" of God upon his life, until finally, in Trinity Term of 1929, he admitted that God was God and knelt to pray. It had been a slow, agonizing process, in which he strove to preserve dominion over his own life and thought. But in the end, he said, he was unable to resist: God had overpowered him!

Malcolm Muggeridge (1903–1990), the British journalist, film-maker, and social commentator, was another famous convert from agnosticism. He told in a book called *Jesus Rediscovered* how for years he believed in the dream of socialist reforms, but finally surrendered to Christ after seeing him in all the poor people on the streets. He was in Russia at the time, Kiev in the 1930s, and attended an Easter service where the people were packed in like sardines. He was pressed against a stone pillar, scarcely able to breathe. He watched all the peasant faces, illumined by hope as they sang about Christ and how there was no help from anyone but him. Suddenly he realized that Christ was indeed the hope of the world — not social and political reforms, the engineering "miracles" that somehow always seemed to fail the poor, but the ageless Galilean who himself chose poverty and whose name had inspired millions of people through the centuries. Christ, he saw, was the light of the world, the one the darkness had not been able to extinguish. He turned toward this light — the light of love and peace and creativity — and began to follow it. And, as he followed, everything in his life was different.

Years later, when he was in India making a documentary movie about Mother Teresa, Muggeridge wanted to film her at her pre-dawn prayers. She insisted that there be no bright lights in the chapel, for she was there to pray, not to be seen doing so. Muggeridge ordered the cameramen to remove the lights, but to shoot the scene anyway, even if it was too dark to be used. Back in his studio in England, he said he was startled when he viewed the segment of film from the chapel to find that it was brilliantly illuminated, as though by a heavenly light. The one-time atheist now had no hesitance at all in recognizing a miracle.

This kind of dramatic conversion will probably always be a feature of Christianity and its view of salvation, for there is a dualism at the heart of the religion between dark and light, rebellion and submission, outer courts and inner courts. Most people are converted gradually, or are raised in an atmosphere where they don't actually need a strong conversion. But there will continue to be tales of resistant agnostics or libertines who at some significant juncture of their lives are invaded by the holy presence and suddenly transformed for a new life of service and witness.

Three

Salvation through the Centuries

By now, it should be obvious that the very idea of salvation held by present-day Christians has unfolded through a number of stages across the centuries. In the earliest Hebrew culture, redemption had to do primarily with relief from suffering, protection from enemies, and rescue from death. Even after the Exodus and the giving of the law, says Eric C. Rust in *Salvation History*, the promise of God to his people was understood "more at the material level — a land to dwell in, material plenty, and victory over their enemies."[14]

Sometime in the so-called "intertestamental" period, between the writing of the Old and New Testaments, there accrued to this understanding a concept of life beyond death, as witnessed by the apocalyptic book of Daniel. The Sadducees of Jesus' time, purists who insisted on limiting all doctrine to what was contained in the Torah and nothing more, ridiculed the concept. But the early Christians took up the idea with enthusiasm, and the concept was given extraordinary impetus in their preaching by the fact that their own Savior had been crucified, was dead and buried, and had risen from the grave.

Christian apologists combed the Hebrew scriptures for "evidences" that Christ and his atonement were part of God's plan for his people from the beginning. Christian theology, at the outset, consisted mainly of constructing, or at least rewriting, Hebrew theology to include its own Redeemer. According to Walter Brueggemann in *Theology of the Old Testament:* "Old Testament theology has been characteristically a Christian enterprise, for it is a Christian, as distinct from a Jewish, propensity to think in large, systematic theological categories."[15] Much of the theological enterprise of the New Testament is taken up with prooftexting — lifting supposed references from their original settings and using them to "proclaim" Christ, to prove that the prophets, in particular, actually foretold the coming of Christ and the culmination of all God's promises in him.

For the next two thousand years, from the time of Christ to the present, life after death became one of the central doctrines of Christian proclamation. How to secure that life, however, frequently became a matter of heated and even deadly conflict. Anyone who thinks that the church has always held a single opinion of the nature of salvation is grossly mistaken. That too has been the subject of frequent controversy and gradual development.

It is important to remember that Christianity burst forth in a culture, or number of cultures, where communication was often difficult, if not altogether impossible. Historians sometimes say that Christianity was born at a propitious time — the *kairotic* moment — when communication in the ancient world was at its acme, and that is possibly true. The Roman government did well, for its day, in tying the ends of its far-flung empire together. It built roads almost everywhere, provided for safe shipping, and had a system of couriers and message delivery that was, at the time, state-of-the-art. But letters often took months to reach their destinations, if indeed they got there at all. And travel, for all its "modern" conveniences, was still painfully slow and arduous. Branches of the church that sprang up in out-of-the-way locations around the empire were seldom in touch with other churches. Their understandings of the gospel and its ramifications were as varied and uncollated as their news of the world in general.

Consider the fact that there was not even a standardization of New Testament scriptures until about the year 200 CE. Until then, the churches in the widespread Christian world used whatever texts they liked as the basis of their theology, including locally developed writings that were often weird, erratic, and filled with incredible stories.

As evidence of this, we have the batch of manuscripts discovered in 1945 in the Nag Hammadi region of Egypt. Two brothers digging for nitrates to fertilize their crops happened upon a large clay vessel containing eight volumes of hand-copied texts from an ancient Christian community. The manuscripts, translated from Greek into Coptic, the local language, contained an amazing number and variety of writings, including, among others, "The Gospel of Truth," "The Apocryphon of John," "The Gospel of Thomas," "The Gospel of the Egyptians," "The Apocalypse of Adam," "The Gospel of Mary," and "The Sophia of Jesus Christ."

Scholars have been poring over these tractates ever since, learning a great deal about the kind of writings that obviously sprang up like weeds all over the Christian map. They contain an incredible diversity, from secret sayings of Jesus in "The Gospel of Thomas," such as "Love your brother like your soul, guard him like the pupil of your eye," to the Gnostic "Treatise on the Resurrection," which has Jesus transforming himself at the resurrection into "an imperishable Aeon" and swallowing "the visible by the invisible."[16]

The Nag Hammadi community was obviously a Gnostic settlement. Gnosticism, in both its Christian and non-Christian versions, was widespread in the Roman empire, and it reached its peak in the middle of the second century under such famous teachers as Basilides of Alexandria and Valentinus of Rome. Believing that matter is evil, the Gnostics considered the story of Christ, who came from beyond the world, very attractive. But they usually denied that Jesus was truly human, and thus posed a problem for Christians who considered his humanity essential to their Christology. According to the Gnostics, salvation is through a special kind of knowledge, or *gnosis*, which is mystical or transcendental in nature. When people receive this knowledge, they are instantly victorious over the evil world of matter. In my opinion, the so-called "messianic secret" in the Gospel of Mark is a Gnostic element, for it is the mystery that causes those who are capable of receiving it suddenly to triumph over the world around them.

Another kind of Christianity extremely popular in the second century was Montanism, which took its name from a Phrygian priest named Montanus. By the end of the first century, many churches were already using the trinitarian formula to baptize people — that is, in the name of the Father, Son, and Holy Spirit. The Gospel of John represented Jesus as promising to send his

Spirit on believers, empowering them to live more dynamically than they presently did. As the second century dawned and Jesus had not returned, many began to wonder if the predictions of his coming were exaggerated. Montanus declared that Jesus' Spirit had come and was speaking to him. The period of the Christ was over, he said, and the period of the Spirit had begun. People should fast, eat no meat, practice asceticism, and remain celibate in order to attract the Spirit to their lives.

Great numbers of Christians who were disenchanted with the worldliness of their surroundings flocked to these teachings, and many followed Montanus's direction to move to Phrygia to await the end of the world.

Yet another very popular group in the second century was the Marcionites, followers of Marcion, a wealthy Roman Christian. Marcion was strongly influenced by the Gnostics, and he believed that Jesus represented a good world that was in opposition to the evil world he had entered. Even the God of the Old Testament, declared Marcion, was part of the evil world, and was not even connected with the God worshiped by Jesus. Therefore Marcion wanted Christians to abandon the Old Testament completely, keeping only the Gospels and writings of Paul for their guidance. Like Montanus, Marcion counseled asceticism, sexual abstinence, and vegetarianism.

Excommunicated by the more conservative churches in 144 CE, Marcion established a separate church with his numerous followers and compiled a Bible for them that consisted of only ten letters of Paul and the Gospel of Luke. He edited these writings to eliminate all references suggesting that Jesus worshiped the God of the Old Testament as his Father.

As far as anyone knows, this was the first attempt ever made to form a New Testament canon. As a result, the other, more orthodox churches realized that it was time for them to develop a canon of their own, and finally, some fifty years later, after numerous conferences and endless negotiations, our present collection of New Testament writings came into being and the canon was closed.

There were of course numerous other "heretical" churches that arose during the formative years of the church as a whole. The sheer diversity of them threatened to overwhelm the Christian movement. Gradually the church began to organize itself along stricter lines, electing officers, holding conferences, and hammering out statements of faith to which most of the churches could and would consent. But the years from the death of Christ to the end of the second century were often wild and tumultuous, owing to the remoteness of most congregations and the number of fanciful theologies that seemed to spread like viruses throughout the empire. It is almost a wonder, when we think about it, that anything like a centralized, orthodox church was able to establish itself in the midst of such a welter of contending ideas and philosophies.

And of course the question always remains, did the right Christians win? The final decisions about belief and orthodoxy were invariably predicated on the three *p*'s — power, politics, and popularity. Did this mean that the Gnostics, the Montanists, the Marcionites, and other heretics were always wrong? Or did they lose merely because they weren't as strong, clever, and numerous as those who voted another way?

The Orthodox View of Salvation

Gradually, orthodox Christianity — which, after Irenaeus, designated itself as catholic (or universal) Christianity — established itself out of the bedlam of conflicting theologies and ideologies. It was a long and arduous process, which, although it may seem discomfiting to think so, continues even today.

By the time of Hippolytus, at the end of the second century, a kind of creed was being used with candidates for baptism that expressed belief in God the Father Almighty; in Christ his Son, who was born of the Holy Spirit and the virgin Mary, was crucified and raised from the dead, ascended into heaven to sit at the Father's right hand, and will come again to judge the quick and the dead; and in "the Holy Spirit, and the Holy Church, and the resurrection of the flesh."

Those who worship in creed-citing churches today will recognize these words as the basis for the Apostles' Creed, which was finalized in its present form some time before the middle of the eighth century, although a nearly perfect representation of it occurred at least as early as the Gallican Creed in the first half of the sixth century.

The other creed widely used in Christendom today is the Nicene Creed, adopted in the fourth century. It was longer and more expansive than the Apostles' Creed because the church at that time was dealing with the so-called *Logos* controversy, in which a substantial number of Christians rejected the Gospel of John because of its passage declaring, "In the beginning was the Word (*Logos*), and the Word was with God, and the Word was God" (John 1:1). The Nicene Creed said that Jesus was "of one substance with the Father," that all things both in heaven and on earth were made through him, and that "for our salvation [he] came down and was made flesh."

Many of the opponents of the *Logos* theology were known as Monarchians because they insisted that only God himself was Lord of all (as a monarch) and that Jesus was God's Son by adoption, not because he existed forever (thus denying the trinity). But the opponents were outvoted at Nicaea and the preexistence of Christ was upheld as the orthodox doctrine.

As a result of its struggles with various dissenting opinions, the church became increasingly organized during the third century, with more and more authority being vested in its bishops. The priesthood assumed more importance in local congregations, and the authority of the priests over the laity was more meticulously delineated. The bishoprics rigorously controlled entry into the priesthood, and ordination was viewed as one of the major sacraments of the church, along with baptism, confirmation, the Lord's Supper, penance, extreme unction, marriage, and, until the Council of Trent in 1545 identified these in particular, many other "channels" of invisible grace.

As the church assumed more and more priestly control over the various means of grace, it became in effect the retailer of salvation, meting out redemption according to rules and regulations established by the bishops in council, and the idea of conversion that had been so central to the early church gradually gave way to a kind of automatic inclusion in the body of Christ and participation in grace through the sacraments. In some sense, at least, the kingdom of God became institutionalized, so that, especially after Constantine's adoption of Christianity as the official religion of the Roman Empire after 325 CE, the future of the church was assured, but at the price of the passion and spirituality of its earlier incarnation.

What did salvation look like to the majority of Christians in the Middle Ages? To a large extent, it looked like the church itself. People found comfort in the almost universally agreed-upon regimen of sacraments, holy days, and saints' tales that explained their world and regulated their entrance into heaven. Their local priests administered everything with an eye to tradition and the blessings of Rome — or, in the case of the Eastern Church, Constantinople. Children were baptized into church membership soon after birth. When old enough to understand, they were instructed in the essentials of the faith, confirmed, and permitted to share in the Eucharist. When they married, they did so under the aegis of the priest and the church. They confessed their sins regularly to the priest and accepted the penance imposed for forgiveness. During Lent, they underwent special privations to remind them of their fealty to God, and at Easter they rejoiced, received communion, and witnessed the baptism of those who had been born during the preceding year. When they became ill or appeared to be dying, they received the special rites that would ease their passage into the presence of God and the holy angels.

Their whole lives were essentially "covered" by the grace of God in this orderly manner, and, if the methodology allowed them to become careless or slipshod about faith, which Martin Luther and other Reformers would contend, it was nevertheless a comfortable culture for accepting life and the future on their own terms.

The Reformers' View of Salvation

Luther of course began life as a Roman Catholic and became an Augustinian monk. But several things bothered him about the ease with which people at the end of the Middle Ages wore the cloak of their religion. One was the incredible worldliness of the papacy in Rome, where self-indulgence among priests and popes had become the accepted way of life. Didn't Christ live as a poor man and instruct his followers to care for the poor? Another was the automatic way most Christians received their means of grace, without true repentance and humility.

Luther was particularly disturbed by the flagrant sale of indulgences — written decrees pardoning people for sins — by the pope's representatives who were trying to raise money to pay for St. Peter's, the incredibly expensive new basilica in Rome.

He was also unhappy that his own religious practices, ardent though they were, had not brought him peace of soul nor had they delivered him from fears of natural threats such as thunderstorms — he had had a particularly harrowing experience in a violent storm — and eternal damnation. In the end, his preparation for teaching Paul's letter to the Romans to young monks convinced him that true Christianity was more about faith in God's grace than about the kind of neatly packaged salvation his church offered.

Perhaps, under a different pope, the papacy and its councils might have heard the young Augustinian with more courtesy, appointed him to meet with the bishops on a regular basis to discuss matters with them, and thus generally assuaged his growing unhappiness with the church. But that didn't happen. And if it hadn't been Luther who precipitated a full-scale rebellion within the church, it would have been someone else.

Reformation had been brewing for a long time, at least since the rise of the Dominican and Franciscan orders of mendicant preachers in the thirteenth century, whose message and lifestyle often challenged Rome's lack of spirituality. In the fourteenth century, the teaching of Thomas Bradwardine, an Oxford theologian, drawing a clear distinction between the grace of God and the lack of merit in all human beings, became widespread and influential, paving the way for Luther's own writings about faith and works. Later, John Wyclif, who also taught at Oxford, became convinced that the Bible, not the church, is the only arbiter of faith, and he was instrumental in translating the New Testament from the Latin of the Vulgate into English. His followers, sent out in pairs like the Franciscans, were highly successful with the common people. Too successful, in fact, for Rome's comfort. Following a peasant's revolt in 1381, Wyclif's opinions were condemned and his Lollards, or "poor priests," were arrested.

The climate, in other words, was right for reforming the church. The whole world was in social upheaval following the Black Death and the political wars of the fourteenth and fifteenth centuries. The new humanism of Nicholas de Cusa, Jacques Le Fèvre, Johannes Reuchlin, and Desiderius Erasmus was prodding theologians to redefine their faith. Universities were springing up everywhere — twelve in Germany alone during the fifteenth century. The Renaissance's general emphasis on a return to documentary sources mandated that closer attention be paid to Christianity's biblical origins. Mystical piety was springing up all over Europe, contesting the profligacy and self-indulgence of the pope and his bishops.

When Luther tacked his Ninety-Five Theses on the castle door at Wittenberg as a proposal for discussion — at the time, it was actually nothing more — the crack of the hammer was like the tap on a goblet at the critical moment when the water within is ready to become ice. Voilà! It turned the religious world on its head, and suddenly there were not only Luther but Karlstadt, Melancthon, Zwingli, Calvin, Knox, Hubmaier, Jacob Hut, Münzer, and dozens of others clamoring for a reexamination of everything Christians professed to believe. And many of them were far more radical than Luther!

As the Reformers investigated biblical sources to reestablish the meaning of faith, the primary thing that became clear to all of them was that Christ had come to establish a personal relationship between the believer and God, one that did not require the mediation of the church and its sacraments for fulfillment. Christ died to save sinners, and it was not up to the pope and bishops of the church to decide who would be redeemed and who wouldn't.

Once more, the Pauline note of salvation by grace through faith in God rang out clearly and emphatically in the Christian community. A tear suddenly occurred in the entire fabric of Western society. To many devout Catholics, it must have seemed as if they were living in the end times, and only the return of Christ himself would restore peace and order to their world.

Because of the primacy of the biblical word in the Reformers' thought, new translations of the scriptures began appearing everywhere, along with thousands of tractates and books expounding the meaning of the texts. It has been said that every major advance in technology produces a new wave of culture, and the employment of movable type by Gutenberg in 1453 (the Chinese had invented it earlier) was surely the instrumentation that favored the developments in reformed thinking. Europe and Great Britain were flooded by new information about the Bible and the Christian faith. The Bible became the Reformers' authority, over the authority of the pope and his council in the church, and we are still witnessing the effect of this every time we turn on the television set and behold an independent preacher espousing a vigorous interpretation of some scriptural text.

Salvation, under the Reformers' zeal, was identified no longer with the sacraments of baptism and the Lord's Supper, administered by the church, but with the individual's repentance for sin and acceptance of the grace of God, which offers perpetual atonement through the blood of Christ on the cross. No intermediary is needed. Christ's mission, in fact, was interpreted as having been the total subversion of all religious establishments and hierarchies, so that every person has direct and unfettered access to God. Faith alone is the basis of rapprochement with the divine. Any and all ecclesiastical structures, therefore, are in need of constant reexamination to determine whether they are serving the gospel's purpose or merely obscuring it.

Protestantism (from the Latin *pro testare,* "to speak on behalf of," as in a court) was not merely an enemy of the traditional church when it grew fat and abusive of its authority, but an ongoing principle of reform for every era. In its turn, it has worked over Lutherans, Presbyterians, Anglicans, Episcopalians, Methodists, and

Baptists, as well as all the other branches of Christianity. It is the gift that keeps on giving.

A Pandora's Box of Salvation Beliefs

What really happened in the sixteenth century, with the resounding success of the reformation movement, was the opening of a virtual Pandora's box of religious opinions. Individualism flourished. It was not always easy. Even the Protestant churches retained a sense of the medieval church's traditional authority and responsibility to punish heretics. The death of Miguel Servetus, the Spanish author of *De Trinitatis Erroribus*, at the hands of Calvin's followers in Geneva is the most famous case in point, but everywhere, from Europe to the shores of the American colonies, people suffered for disagreeing with whatever religious viewpoint was locally honored. Still, there was a heady sense of individual prerogative in the air, and this was to remain the case to the present day.

What is sometimes overlooked is the number of experiments and reformations the movement occasioned within the Roman Catholic Church itself. In Venice, Bruccioli's Italian translation of the New Testament was published in 1530, and the whole Bible in 1532, making the Bible available to Italians as Luther's translation had done for Germans. A high-ranking Spaniard named Juan Valdés formed a society of evangelical mystics in the city of Naples, and one of Valdés's disciples, Benedetto of Mantua, produced an extremely popular book called *The Benefits of Christ's Death*, calling for obeisance, not to the church, but to Christ. Out of renewed Spanish devotionalism came the remarkable figure of Ignatius of

Loyola, the former soldier who founded the organization known as the Society of Jesus, or the Jesuits.

Ignatius's *Spiritual Exercises*, an enormously influential work, enlists the human imagination and even dreams to enable its user to examine himself, renounce sin, and become an ardent follower of Christ. Even though it was intended to promote obedience to the Church of Rome, the book's emphasis on individualism was very modern and allowed the Society of Jesus to become extremely powerful, even to this day, as a creative and intellectual wing of the church.

The breakup of medieval culture brought about by the Black Death and consequent changes in the social fabric of Europe, together with the rise of the modern state and the development of a monetary system, led to an outburst of exploration and colonization. This, combined with the new devotionalism of both Protestant and Catholic churches, produced a frenzy of missionary activity in which fervent, God-fearing explorers carried the Christian faith to people in faraway places who had never heard of Jesus and his death on the cross. The new colonies in eastern North America were largely dominated by the Protestants, but the Catholics were extremely active in establishing new missions in Central and South America, as well as in Canada. And both groups planted the seeds of Christian faith in several areas of the Far East.

In Europe, meanwhile, the new science was beginning to compel a rethinking of many Christian ideas, especially in astronomy. Nicolaus Copernicus, a Pole, published his speculations on a heliocentric universe, which after his death were given further elucidation by Tycho Brahe and Johann Kepler. Galileo Galilei, the Italian scientist who invented the thermometer and developed the pendulum, applied the use of the telescope to the study of the heavens and conclusively validated Copernicus's ideas. Sir Isaac Newton of England, in his famous *Principia,* used mathematical formulas to prove that the motions of the planets are the result of gravitational pull. The so-called Copernican Revolution, which displaced the earth from the center of the universe, had a profound effect on the faith of many believers, producing a fervor for scientific inquiry that frequently led to expressions of agnosticism.

Out of the scientific movement grew a new interest in philosophy that would also have a widespread effect on Christianity. René Descartes in France, Baruch Spinoza in the Netherlands, Gottfried Wilhelm Leibniz in Germany, and John Locke and David Hume in England were all applying rational understanding to such subjects as the human mind, the nature of God, and the way God interacts with the world. Faith was no longer regarded as a subject owned by the church and thus sheltered from rigorous questioning and investigation.

And of course one of the most profound challenges to faith and organized religion was the work of Charles Darwin, the English naturalist, whose publication of *The Origin of the Species* in 1859, based on observations made during a five-year journey to the Far East and South America, is still producing reverberations today in the schools and courts of America. Darwin waited for years to publish his epoch-making book, knowing that it would be highly controversial, and did so finally because he became aware that another scientist was working on similar theories. The public outrage of many churchmen was so vehement that for years

Darwin's wife, Emma, worried that she and her husband would spend eternity in separate destinations.

But Darwin's theory of evolution was only a natural development from the work of Copernicus and Galileo, and part of the long and sometimes painful process of desacralizing Christianity's myth of biblical accuracy. It meant that the act of having faith would be different in the future, because it would involve what the nineteenth-century Danish philosopher Søren Kierkegaard would call "the *leap* of faith," a profound, transintellectual commitment to a supreme being, instead of a mere acceptance of the community's endorsement of an ancient system of beliefs.

Years later, in the twentieth century, sociologists would develop the idea of "the social construction of reality," an observable phenomenon whereby human beings are inducted into a complete system of beliefs and understandings by their parents, teachers, and peers. The newborn child is actually a *tabula rasa,* a blank slate, and thereafter imbibes all its information about the world from those who tend it. Children who grow up among the Maoris in New Zealand have a very different concept of the world and religious faith from the concept of those reared in Mexico or Scandinavia or Turkey. The children of Catholics have a different understanding of the church than the children of Protestants. In other words, we are all *programmed* by the significant people in our environment. Even if we grow up with independent spirits and determine to rethink life according to our own carefully gathered information, we can never escape from certain habits of thought and reaction ingrained in us from our beginnings.

In a world like ours, which despite its increasing globalism is still divided into countless local duchies and provinces, there are bound to be an almost infinite number of personal understandings of God, humanity, the world, and salvation. The growth of educational possibilities — books, schools, travel, newspapers, journals, e-communication — suggests that there is probably a greater degree of individuation in these matters than ever before in history. As R. D. Laing said, no two persons can have exactly the same experiences, and, with the multiplicity of options in a large part of the world today, there is concomitantly a heightened sense of particularity.

With that in mind, it is time to talk about salvation and some of its many implications for our lives today.

Four

Salvation in Our Time

Since World War I (in Europe) and World War II (in America), the "acids of modernity," as Walter Lippmann once called them, have been steadily corroding traditional understandings of both faith and salvation. Until then, most of Christendom had a general understanding that salvation meant being rescued from eternal damnation to life with Christ in God. There were certain temperamental and theological differences between Catholics and Protestants, to be sure, and many differences among the various Protestant denominations, but their sermons and books revealed a unanimity of opinion about the end results.

How much weight was given to salvation in this life and how much to salvation in the next life tended to depend on the circumstances of the believers. Frontier dwellers in America, for whom life was always hard, earnest, and uncertain, responded to evangelists' promises of a life to come where the streets would be paved with gold and there would be no more pain or separation. The hymnody they loved was mainly that by Isaac Watts and Charles Wesley about the Cross, redemption, and a very literal heaven, which also fueled the evangelical movement in Great Britain, where coal miners, small land holders, and poor city dwellers formed the backbone of the newly created and widely scorned Methodist movement.

The religion of the African Americans in America was likewise very otherworldly, and its worshipers sang lustily of "crossing over Jordan" and finding rest in "the promised land." It has often been dubbed "escapist" religion, and in many ways it was. But it enabled slaves who owned nothing, not even the clothes on their backs, and who served at the wink and nod of landed gentry and prosperous city-dwellers, to visualize a better existence where they would be valued as real souls and accorded equal status with their present masters.

Well-to-do families in America's nascent metropolitan areas, on the other hand, tended to concentrate more on the moral side of religion, and to dwell on thoughts of the afterlife primarily at wakes and funerals, when the consolation of a life immune to fortune's vicissitudes seemed more important. Many of them regarded religion as a convenient support for the status quo, buttressing the system that made their lives comfortable and enjoyable.

But life for most Americans, not just the favored few, began to improve after the mid-twentieth century. By then, a majority of the people lived in cities and no longer worried about the financial ravages that accompanied a hard drought or a bitter storm. Central heating and air-conditioning allowed them to enjoy their homes in all seasons. Social security and insurance programs alleviated a lot of fears and anxieties normally attached to the retirement years. Advancing medical care, especially in the form of inoculations and antibiotics, rendered plagues and epidemics much less potent. Minimum-wage laws established a modicum of financial security for even menial laborers. With school integration and busing, people in poorer districts could expect educational opportunities for their children comparable to those of most other children. Congress passed legislation guaranteeing equal pay for equal work. As the musical *Oklahoma* put it, "Everything's up to date in Kansas City" and "things have gone about as far as they can go!"

As social welfare improved, the appeal of justice and compensation in another life began to recede in importance. The emphasis in American religion started to shift from eternal salvation to experiencing the good life now. It was only a subtle change, and it did not mean that Americans no longer believed in life after death. In fact, polls consistently showed that at least three-quarters of the populace did believe in an afterlife. But the shift did indicate that the majority of Americans no longer regarded their religion from the same vantage point as most of the world's underprivileged and disadvantaged, a fact often evidenced in books by social ethicists writing from the perspective of poverty-stricken natives in Africa and Central America.

Many preachers on radio and TV announced a gospel of materialism, although most of them were loath to openly say so. Oral Roberts, Robert Tilton, Jim and Tammy Bakker, and many others counseled that all Christians had to do in order to have what they wanted, including fine homes, new cars, and better jobs, was to pray for it. Father Devine, a famous black preacher in New York, drove a limousine, lived like a movie star, and cheerfully assured his congregation that God wanted his people to live that way.

Inevitably, of course, there are still numerous evangelists who regard salvation as a simple matter of turning to the Lord, and they shade their maps of the world to show what vast spaces and masses of people still have not accepted the good news of Jesus Christ. In fact, I wrote this on a Sunday afternoon shortly after my wife and I attended a worship service in a Baptist church where the guest preacher, a young man, was a missionary to a principally Muslim country and harangued us for more than forty-five minutes about how we should be "on fire for the Lord" and truly care about the billions of people who are dying and going to hell because nobody has ever told them about Jesus. He seemed clearly convinced that this is the case, and cited many scriptural texts to prove his point.

My wife and I talked about this over lunch, and said how disconnected we felt from the young man's point of view. My wife said she could remember only one time when she ever heard me preach a sermon from a similar point of view, and that was when I was only eighteen years old and just beginning my career as a minister.

"But think how you changed before you were as old as this man," she added.

It was true. During that ten-year period, I earned master's and doctor's degrees in English literature, received my ministerial training at Harvard, and spent two years as a professor and dean of the chapel at a liberal arts college. I shuddered to think that I had ever been as cocksure of everything as the young man I'd heard that morning, and I wondered if there was anything, even a few years in graduate school, that could possibly unsettle him in his obvious commitment to a literal reading of the scriptures.

But while the traditional evangelical notion of salvation as re-demption from eternal punishment continues to enjoy popularity in certain religious circles in America, it is also apparent that a major shift has been taking place in the thinking of many Chris-tians. It is a shift that began with a widespread acceptance of the contention of more liberal teachers and theologians that the Bible is not literally the Word of God but a collection of all-too-human documents that are often at odds with one another and reflect only a limited, even parochial, understanding of the world and its history.

Once that contention was accepted, it was only a matter of time before people began to question the conclusions of a faith based on a literal reading of the scriptures. If God is a God of love, for example, then why, in the Old Testament, did he so frequently order the Hebrews to annihilate their enemies, and why, in the New Testament, did he set such store by the conversion of pagans? Couldn't he, like the supernal parent he is, rise above the sins of *all* his children, not merely those who cleared the hurdles established by the first Christians and their successors in the earliest centuries of the church?

I think Jerry Falwell is right about the "slippery slope." I once asked him, across a lunch table, why he couldn't accept people as Christians if they said that the Bible wasn't verbatim the Word of God. He declined to give a full answer to the question, but he said it all had to do with "starting down the slippery slope."

I say that I think he was right. That *is* the big issue for all Christians, whether the Bible is literally true or only morally and provisionally true. Once a person accepts the arguments of the critics — that, *one,* there are no extant original manuscripts of the

biblical books; *two,* there are many discrepancies and disagree-
ments among the later manuscripts we do possess; *three,* there
are plainly contradictory statements and arrangements in the ac-
counts of the four Gospels (for example, Jesus' act of driving the
money-changers out of the temple occurs near the end of his ministry in the synoptics but at the beginning in the Gospel of John);
and, *four,* there are almost certainly textual additions and emen-
dations made by editors who handled the texts after the original
authors — that person cannot help undertaking a journey of reason and discovery that will lead to altered viewpoints on many
subjects related to the Bible and Christian theology.

If it is not a slippery slope, it is at least a broad set of steps
leading inexorably away from a large number of religious opinions
that depend for their continued existence on the unchallenged
authority of the biblical text.

At a recent conference of ministers in a Southern state, I asked
the question, during a discussion period, "How do you regard salvation in your own lives?" There was silence for a moment. Then
one minister said, "For me, it is a matter of attaining the fullness of myself, of becoming everything I ought to become, and of
enjoying the satisfaction of having done so."

I offered the comment that he had said nothing about life after
death. Again there was a pause.

"I suppose," he said at last, "that is because I am uncertain
about life after death. I know what the Bible says, but that is only
figurative in nature, not the way it will literally be. What I do
know about is my own life in the here-and-now, and what 'being
saved' means to it."

As the others spoke, it became plain that they were substantially in agreement with the first minister. The terms they used included such words as "self-realization," "self-fulfillment," "satisfactory achievement," and "harmonious relationship," most of which come from the field of psychology and can be found in hundreds of self-help works available in any bookstore.

One minister made a few remarks about his appreciation of the Buddhist idea of "mindfulness" — being blissfully aware of life as a whole and thus not becoming overly elated by good happenings or depressed by bad ones. To him, this was a satisfactory description of what it means to be saved.

Admittedly, these ministers were not biblical literalists, or at least, any who might have been remained secretive about it. But neither were they theological liberals or radicals. Most of them belonged to the Cooperative Baptist Fellowship, a moderate group of Southern Baptists who in the last several years have established a counter-movement in protest of the fundamentalist takeover of their old denomination. They still preach from the Bible every Sunday, still support missionary efforts to evangelize the world, and, theoretically at least, still confess their faith along mostly traditional lines.

But in a meeting without lay people present, as fellow pastors who could be completely open and honest, they admitted that they no longer conceive of salvation the way they once did, but in humbler, more tentative terms.

"Do you believe the lost are going to hell?" I asked one minister afterward.

"Perhaps," he told me. "But not to the kind of hell people once believed in. A kind of purgatory, perhaps; a lackluster place for souls that are ill-defined, that never found their real purpose for being."

Did this particular minister feel robbed or deprived of something that once made his religion more dramatic and himself a more tireless evangelist?

He smiled. "Not really. I guess I'm not the stem-winder I was when I was a young man. But I'm very happy with my view of things now. I feel more integrated — and far more in touch with reality."

Was he just as convinced of an afterlife as before?

"Oh, yes," he said. "I just don't know what it will be like. But it doesn't matter. I have enough faith in God to leave that up to him."

Corroborative Voices

Later, as I pondered what I had heard from these ministers, I wondered whether their understanding of salvation had become the general one among both evangelical and nonevangelical ministers in the U.S. So I wrote to a few clergy in various parts of the country, being careful to choose persons who not only would respond thoughtfully but would represent different parts of the national religious spectrum.

What I heard from them confirmed what I suspected after my visit with the ministers at the conference. They all conformed to what Elizabeth Lesser calls "the new spirituality." In the "old spirituality," she says, God, and the way to worship him, have already been defined and all we need to do is follow the directions. But in the "new spirituality," we listen within for our own definitions of how we shall relate to God. Our deeper longings are our most dependable compass as we search for the truth.[17]

One minister, P. P., who is also a newspaper columnist, was originally a Southern Baptist because his father was a Southern Baptist minister. Eventually he became a Pentecostal because he decided that Pentecostals lived their faith more openly and honestly and were more open to miracles than other Christians. His own conversion, he believes, was a miracle. Jesus figured prominently in his conversion from being "a self-centered drunken wastrel" to becoming a genuine follower.

Yet he said, "The older I get, the less I'm sure exactly what it means to say that 'Jesus saves.' Jesus didn't come just to save souls from hell." As Jesus said when he read from the scroll of Isaiah in the synagogue, he came to "grant deliverance here and now, on earth — to open blind eyes and heal broken hearts."

During his lifetime, said this man, he has met all kinds of Christians — those who claim an instant conversion because of a dramatic experience, those who have known Jesus "almost from infancy," and those who say their transformations were "gradual, day-by-day awakenings." So he doesn't value one method of salvation over another. And he is not convinced that a person has to be a Christian in order to be saved.

Some — "certain Jews and Muslims and Buddhists" — he thinks might be saved. "I don't know. It's too big for me."

The only thing he's certain of is his own experience of salvation that began one night in his bedroom when he asked Jesus for help and Jesus "saved" him — an experience that has been growing ever since.

A Presbyterian, B. H., said that she still held in her heart "that simple, revealing experience" of Christ she received as a youngster, but she has grown enormously beyond the understanding of it she possessed then. "Through all these years, my horizon has greatly widened, creating greater understanding and openness."

Whereas she once found the explanation of her salvation simple and easy to talk about, she now finds it impossible to reduce to mere words. But the mysteriousness, she said, "only makes it all the more exciting and challenging."

D. B. C., a Disciples of Christ minister, remembered his childhood experience of accepting Jesus, but said now that "the true mark of salvation is not the act of accepting Jesus, but the divine grace with which we face our moments of desperation and helplessness." Our inability to accept the grace of God, which is there for us unconditionally, robs us of "the inner peace that salvation is all about."

Churches, he thinks, are basically in the "rules" business, making and enforcing the rules they want people to live by. This leads to a lot of anger and misunderstanding, so that churches are not the "true sanctuaries" they were intended to be. Instead of giving people peace, they raise their stress levels.

"Salvation," said D. T., a Presbyterian minister, "is God present in the world with responsive love, drawing all things to God." God starts it, God sustains it, God completes it. We only participate in it and enjoy it.

D. L., a religion reporter who has interviewed and written about people of faith for thirty years, said that he doesn't believe salvation and an afterlife are limited to Christians. Salvation, he thinks, is something that "enfolds" everyone from birth but needs to be realized before it can become truly active in the person's life.

"The moment of salvation," he wrote, arrives "when a person realizes that his or her life, however flawed it may seem, is actually part of a great overall plan and can serve a divine purpose."

D. H., a Presbyterian minister, likewise preferred to believe that salvation is an interfaith matter and belongs to everyone who can only conceive of possessing it. Jesus' life, death, and resurrection, he said, are the center of it for him; but redemption doesn't belong to Christians alone. "It has been and is the purpose of God," he wrote, "to save the whole human race."

In his case, it was Jesus who awakened his consciousness of this. But other spiritual persons may do the same for people in other cultures.

"Salvation," he believes, "is synonymous with health and wholeness and personhood. To be saved means to accept the forgiveness of God, to strive to be a loving, benevolent, redemptive, and forgiving person, and to live relatively free from wanton sin, futility, hatred, resentment, and other infirmities that inhibit wholeness."

This kind of definition does not rule out Buddhists, Hindus, Muslims, or even nonreligious persons.

"I cannot define in any detail what any of this means," this minister continued. "To me, allowing such things as salvation, eternal life, and the nature of God to remain mysteries makes them all the more intriguing, exciting, and wonderful."

P. L., a United Methodist minister in the east, agreed that salvation is not a Christian matter alone. Therefore, he believes, whatever we say about it must be couched in language that would be acceptable in other religions as well.

"For me," he said, "salvation means finding oneself and a higher power, whether we call the higher power the Creator, the Ground of Being, or whatever, and *making peace with both.*" It means "accepting our imperfections and those of others, and knowing that we are all created in love by a supreme being who cherishes everyone."

This translates, the minister went on to say, into having "a compassionate view of all creation" and wanting to relieve the suffering of others. It means that we are to be "healers instead of destroyers." It means "uniting everything and not trying to set up divisions."

J. M., an interdenominational minister and professional counselor, was likewise humble about making any iron-clad definitions. "I struggle with my own faith," he said, "and whenever I try to define it, the definition eludes me."

"Salvation," he wrote, "is about freedom, sometimes passionate, joyous freedom, sometimes a frightening freedom." Unfortunately, he thinks, organized religion often crimps or destroys this freedom. "The more detailed the instructions get, the more restrictive they are, and the more humanly created they are rather than God-given.

"There's a road ahead, sometimes clear, often ill-defined," continued this minister. "Some seeking salvation make it like an organized group tour, while it is really meant as a pilgrimage, a journey to explore unknown territory."

Jesus, he thinks, is not a tour guide but a strong companion for the journey. "Salvation does not really bring answers; it brings a better set of questions."

"I have changed a great deal over the last fifty years," writes
F. C. H., a United Methodist minister in the midwest — "from
black to white. Well, maybe just gray. I am still on my way."

First, he said, it is important to remove heaven and hell from
the picture altogether — these are only "mythical places" that
have become far too important in our thinking about salvation.

Second, we need to realize that having our sins forgiven isn't
the way to achieve redemption. "Getting rid of guilt is a psychological problem, not a religious one." Sin is against other people,
and maybe ourselves, but not against God. The idea that it is
against God is only an invention of the priesthood.

The center of salvation, he said, is the kingdom of God, which
Jesus said is here and now, not in some future time and place.
Jesus taught us in the Lord's Prayer to pray that things on earth
might become like things in heaven. He wanted us to see that
God is tied up with life *now,* and to live our lives accordingly, as
citizens of God's kingdom.

F. H. H., a pastor and teacher in a conservative seminary in
the South, believes that salvation is more interrelational than
most people realize; it transcends the lives of individuals and
has to do with the interactions among them in community and
society. "God is helping us to become better and more fulfilled
people, and in the life to come God will bring us to our true destiny of union with God and community, and with all of God's
creation."

Again and again, in the responses from these ministers, there
is an emphasis on *salvation as wholeness and fulfillment.*

One minister, D. A., a popular Southern Baptist writer, said
that because salvation has to do with being whole he has to think

of it in relation to its opposite, which, in the biblical term, is "perishing." "To perish," he said, "is to have all the aspects of life present but to have nothing to hold the pieces together." It is to live in a fragmented state, "whether through willful dissipation or negligent disregard."

"Salvation," he said, "is the 'glue' that holds life together. It is a relationship with God that provides meaning, opens the door to loving contact with others, and points the way to moral stability. It is never a program or a formula to remember and recite. Instead, it is the force that holds all the confluences of life together."

He cited J. B. Phillips's translation of Colossians 1:17, which speaks of Christ as "the first principle and the upholding principle of the whole scheme of creation."

God's desire from the beginning, said this minister, is that we should be *coherent* in him — that, as the Apostle Paul put it, everything in our lives should "hold together" for us. If we aren't saved, or in the process of being saved, we are simply *incoherent.*

It is very interesting that almost every minister from whom I heard was very conscious of world religions and the importance of defining salvation in a way that could include non-Christians.

Kenneth Woodward, who for forty years was the extraordinarily perceptive religion editor of *Newsweek* magazine, has said in a public lecture on the nature of the religious pilgrimage that any true spiritual journey now demands "a personal encounter with religions other than our own."[18]

Woodward recommended a practice that he tried to follow as an editor, which was a method espoused by Father John Dunne of Notre Dame in his book *The Way of All the Earth.* Dunne calls

for "passing over to the other by way of sympathetic understanding" — something he has done with the lives of the founders of all
the great religious traditions — and then returning to one's own
religion with renewed insight and understanding.

Woodward admitted that he was often in disagreement with
evangelical Christians, because evangelicals, he said, proudly
sponsor "a conservative kind of Christianity that really does not
conserve much of the Christian tradition," and are thus guilty of
"a flight to premature certainty." He praised Thomas Merton and
Dorothy Day for their remarkable spiritual journeys, despite the
fact that they seldom actually traveled anywhere, but remarked of
Billy Graham, who traveled constantly, that "he never really went
anywhere as a genuine pilgrim."

Graham's problem, in Woodward's opinion, was "that he was
already saved and so had nothing to learn from others that was
of any importance in his relationship to God."

I think Woodward put his finger on the difference between most
of the ministers I consulted and their counterparts in the most
conservative or fundamentalist circles. Those who wrote me all
regarded their lives as being on pilgrimage, with something yet to
learn — in some cases a great deal — whereas their counterparts
would probably say that they already have everything they need
and are therefore not interested in seeking anything else.

This is a dichotomy that is likely to continue in Christianity, as
in other religions. There will always be some pilgrims who are constantly seeking something higher, other, and more fulfilling, while
there will also be those who disdain such seeking, maintaining that
it disregards and even dishonors what they have already received.

While I can hardly claim any real neutrality in the matter, I believe that the future of religion always belongs to the pilgrims, not to those who decide to stay at home, content with what they have already received. Regardless of the pockets of resistance, every religion undergoes certain irresistible transformations, usually along the obvious lines of cultural change. When mutations occur in the world around us, something inevitably happens to the way we believe and see ourselves believing, however stubbornly we intend to remain as we were.

Those who have confessed to shifts in their theology during the last half-century are probably a far better guide to the future of soteriological opinion than the masses of conservative Christians who continue to insist on holding to outdated religious formulas.

"Christians are slowly learning to welcome 'otherness,' religious, cultural, and otherwise," says theologian Harvey Cox of Harvard University, "not as an inconvenience we must somehow put up with but as a gift of God, a reminder of our human finitude and of the unsearchable richness of the Holy One."[19]

I agree, and I see this as an indication of where our faith and understanding are headed in the decades ahead. The ministers in my sampling are not really unusual at all; they are harbingers of the future, of where Christianity as a whole is going, despite any automated messages from the more conservative side of things.

There is a "wholeness hunger in our general culture," as historian Wade Clark Roof puts it. "It is something felt by many people, something that underlies comments about 'centering your life' and 'finding connections' that are so frequently voiced in the populace at large."[20] And, as usual, culture is driving religion, not the other way around. Ministers and congregations alike are changing their views on salvation and religion in general because everybody in the global village — everybody, at least, except the fundamentalist holdouts — is experiencing the same unconscious urge toward wholeness and acceptance.

Perhaps the evangelicals can see something positive in this — that Jesus, who stands so indisputably at the center of their religion, freed us from the self-centeredness of religion in his day, not so that we could become self-centered in our own way, duplicating what he opposed, but in order that we could be open to the saviors and teachers of all religions, and could say to the people in those religions, "Our Lord has freed us to sit down with you and talk about the things we have in common. Our 'good news' is that we are all on the same pilgrimage, inside what is fast becoming a global village. Why don't we share what we know and listen to one another with the eagerness of those who truly want to trust one another?"

A Personal Testimony

The ministers I have cited expressed my own view as well as theirs. I grew up in a traditionally oriented church — in fact, a fundamentalist church — and accepted the understanding it taught, namely, that Christ had died to save sinners, that salvation meant oneness with Christ now and eternal life after death, and that the highest calling on a person's life is to spread the news of Christ's death and resurrection to the lost so they too may be saved.

One of my favorite hymns as a youth was called "Saved, Saved!"[21] Its chorus proclaimed:

> Saved by His power divine,
> Saved to new life sublime!
> Life now is sweet and my joy is complete,
> For I'm saved, saved, saved!

Each time we sang the word "saved," it was held for a long note, with the final three repetitions of the word rising to an enormous crescendo. I could almost believe I was in heaven when we sang this hymn. In fact, I think everybody in the congregation did, they sang so eagerly.

I won my first convert to Christ when I was sixteen. It was during a revival meeting. Using a list of prospects provided by our minister, a friend and I knocked on the door of a young couple's apartment at eight o'clock in the evening. The knock was answered by a groggy young man clad only in a pair of jeans, who had already gone to bed because he had to be up early in the morning. There, in the dim light from a bulb in the hallway, I explained the plan of salvation to him, my friend and I prayed, and the half-naked young man accepted Christ as his Savior.

The next year, when I was a freshman at Baylor University, I spent Friday nights working in a mission to winos and migrant workers in the grimmest section of Waco, Texas. Almost every week I reported back to mission headquarters at the university the names of two or three men who had been converted to Christ and promised to straighten up their lives.

In those days, I had an image of heaven and hell as actual places, albeit in another dimension from this one, offering eternal reward and punishment. But I have changed a great deal in the last fifty years, a period during which I pastored seven churches and taught at several universities and theological seminaries. I have changed personally, and my views have changed.

I remember when my understanding of salvation and the after-life began to shift. I drew a straight line on the page of a personal journal I was keeping in college. I wrote "God" at one end of the line and "hell" at the other. Heaven, I reasoned, was anywhere God was, and hell — well, hell had to be the opposite of this. It was "not God." It was the absence of the One who gives light and life to everything.

After that simple diagram, I no longer thought of hell in terms of fire and brimstone, as the revivalists in our church had pictured it. I saw it instead as the awful absence of the divine, and I began to believe that all of us, even the best, live at some remove from the beauty and glory of God. Later, when I read Dante's *Inferno* with its various rings or levels of punishment, I remembered my line drawing and realized how I had already located people along the line according to how conscious they were of God's presence.

One day, I realized how impossible it is to imagine what it would be like to be truly in the presence of God — that is, ac-tually to be in heaven. I was a very mystical young man, and liked to contemplate such things. But even in my most insightful moments I couldn't begin to conceive of what it would be like to be totally overwhelmed by divine presence, to be caught up in such an ecstasy of existence that all self-awareness and desire were completely eliminated.

In that moment, I knew that I had gone as far as I could ever go in understanding life after death. I could experiment with literary descriptions of euphoric experience, but I couldn't actually have such an experience. That would have to wait until I died.

I have never ceased to believe in an afterlife, even in my most radically secular moments. Once, when I learned that I had a melanoma cancer and feared that death might be imminent, I actually became quite excited about the prospect of an adventure beyond this present scene. And never at any time in my life have I had the least fear of dying, because I am so convinced of an existence beyond this one that it would be foolish to dread the moment of passage.

But my notion of salvation has been considerably transformed from the simple one I was given as a young Christian. Now, I am quite certain that it is more like what the ministers talked about when they spoke of "self-realization" and "self-fulfillment." It has to do with being so well integrated as a self, so comfortable with the presence of God and the world around me, that I am already in a kind of heaven, even in this highly imperfect world.

I had a dream one night while writing this book that may illustrate what I am saying. I was leading my little two-year-old granddaughter Ellie up the stairs and into a room where I wanted to show her my parents' dog, an Irish terrier, that hulled black walnuts. (Black walnuts, for those unfamiliar with them, are encased in a firm green shell that has a very pungent odor and leaves a semipermanent stain on the hands of anyone who tries to shuck them without gloves.) When we reached the upstairs, my parents were sleeping and vaguely stirring in a bed on one side of the room, while the dog, up on a wooden box on the other side, was busily removing the hulls from a number of walnuts. The floor in front of us was liberally covered with walnuts that had already been hulled.

When I awoke and meditated on this dream, I recognized its meaning almost at once. I was conducting my grandchild into the mysterious presence of my parents, both of whom had been dead for almost a quarter of a century, so there was a kind of "beyond life" quality about the scene. My parents' dog, whose name was Mike (very Irish!), was stationed on a box like the one on which my father used to groom him each day. The walnuts represented a mystery that has always been special to me. Even to this day, when my wife and I are walking in the fall, I will stoop and pick up one or two and carry them with me, sniffing occasionally at their wonderfully pungent odor. And my mind instantly recalled Carl Jung's descriptions of the mandalas we see in our dreams — those special circles that represent fullness and joy in our subconscious. The floor was absolutely littered with these small mandalas!

The dream, in short, was about the many perfect joys of my life — joys that included memories of my parents and a sense of hope and satisfaction in Ellie, my progeny, who bears a strong resemblance to me and will carry on my life force when I have died. I had an extreme sense of blessing, of finding fulfillment in many things — in my lovely wife, my children and grandchildren, my many friends, my writing, my travel, my imagination, my physical vigor, in going to the theater, reading books, exchanging letters and e-mails, and in numerous other things.

In a very real sense, it was a dream about my salvation. Not salvation as I had understood it as a boy and young man, tied to a limited notion of Christ and the kingdom of God. But salvation as I understand it now, as joy and fulfillment and multitudinous gifts, as a deep and abiding sense of inner well-being, as relatedness to everybody and everything around me, as a vision of the absolute richness of human existence, in spite of wars, epidemics, crime, suffering, and human treachery.

I am very fond of David Steindl-Rast's description of salvation as a kind of mental and emotional surprise at this very richness — surprise that the world is as fresh and beautiful as it is. In *Gratefulness, The Heart of Prayer* he speaks of "the powdery bloom on fresh blueberries," and how easy it is to learn to see this.

"It may be," he writes, "that I saw 'this morning morning's minion,' Gerard Manley Hopkins's 'dapple-dawn-drawn falcon in his riding,' or simply it may be this morning's inch of toothpaste on my brush. Both are equally amazing to the eyes of the heart, for the greatest surprise is that there is anything at all — that we are here."[22]

We can cultivate such a sense of amazement, says Steindl-Rast, seeing with "the eyes of our eyes," so that we "begin to see everything as a gift." Everything — the blueberries, the birds in the sky, our wondrous bodies, the people around us — is gift, offering, treat, benefaction, inheritance. Talk about a promised land — the world is our promised land!

This understanding, I am sure, is strongly connected to what the New Testament calls "love" — *agape* love, as distinguished from *eros* love — a totally selfless love that transcends all egotistic desires, a love that radiates out from one's center as surely as energy radiates out from the sun. It is, I am convinced, the real aim of all the biblical injunctions to follow Christ, to keep the commandments, to adhere to the narrow path, to choose light over darkness, to be spiritually faithful to the end. Love is the new nature of every truly converted soul, only it is not new at all, but a reordering of the inner being of the person so that what was there from the beginning is enabled to triumph over everything that would diminish it.

In that sense, salvation does involve integration, self-realization, recovery of a lost order, or the complete reconfiguration of one's being. It means being so totally transformed that one naturally loves everyone and everything, wishes no one any harm, and desires the radical transformation of the whole world and universe, so it may all enjoy the ecstasy one is experiencing in oneself.

This is part of what James Hillman was trying to say in *The Soul's Code*, about being turned around "in the eddies and shallows of meaninglessness" and brought "back to feelings of destiny." It is the feelings of destiny, he thinks, that are lost in so many contemporary lives, and it was to resurrect these feelings that he wrote his book. Most people, he says, dull their lives by the way they conceive them, by not understanding what their fulfillment could mean.[23]

I can feel very sad about the spectacle of great crowds of believers who think that they are converted and saved, but who are still disturbed or angry about many things and would like to see their enemies burned in hell. What did Jesus say about the scribes and Pharisees? "You cross sea and land to make a single disciple, and you make the new convert twice as much a child of hell as yourselves" (Matthew 23:15). There are so many twisted, tormented people who assume, by the definitions they have been taught, that they are saved. Yet their very attitudes, their demeanors, belie their conversions. In their visible distrust of everything that doesn't follow their own blueprints for godliness and order, they are almost pathologically deficient in love and joy.

As a pastor, I met many such unfortunate souls in my parishes. They would come to me insisting that so-and-so was not a good Christian and shouldn't be allowed to take communion, or that I wasn't spending enough time in my sermons condemning what the young people were doing, or that the church shouldn't allow certain groups to use their parlor for meetings. I could almost invariably tell, from the torment in their faces and the anguish in their voices, that there wasn't enough real salvation in their hearts to fill a thimble. Not even a very small thimble. The truly converted folks, on the other hand, never got upset with fellow church members or had a bad word to say about anyone. The sun shone out of their faces when they talked, and it was obvious that they were happy to be living in the spirit of God.

A Word of Caution

I have to keep reminding myself that this is *my* understanding of salvation and the understanding I am seeing in many ministers and reflective lay persons in our country, but it is not an understanding shared by all Christians of more conservative dispositions, particularly in other parts of the world.

Philip Jenkins, Professor of History and Religious Studies at Pennsylvania State University, says that, while educated Christians in America and Western Europe often accept the technological revolution of our era as the sign of an impending theological revolution that will have even more far-reaching results on our lives than the Reformation had on the lives of people in the sixteenth century, the newly minted Christians in other parts of the globe are more likely to be like the early Christians, and not at all like us.

"If we look beyond the liberal West," he says, "we see that another Christian revolution, quite different from the one being called for in affluent American suburbs and upscale urban parishes, is already in progress. Worldwide, Christianity is actually moving toward supernaturalism and neo-orthodoxy, and in many ways toward the ancient world view expressed in the New Testament: a vision of Jesus as the embodiment of divine power, who overcomes the evil forces that inflict calamity and sickness upon the human race."

In the Third World, says Jenkins, "huge and growing Christian populations — currently 480 million in Latin America; 360 million in Africa; and 313 million in Asia, compared with 260 million in North America — now make up what the Catholic scholar Walbert Buhlmann has called the Third Church, a form of Christianity as distinct as Protestantism or Orthodoxy, and one that is likely to become dominant in the faith."[24]

Jenkins is right, of course. The great sweeping changes brought about by the success of Christian missions in Africa, Asia, and Central and South America is producing a force that will impact upon the world as cataclysmically in the near future as Christianity did on the Roman empire in the early centuries, and it is quite different in character from the kind of atmospheric changes I am describing in North American soteriology. There, in Third World Christianity, salvation is still regarded in the old sense, as conversion to Christ and adhering to discipleship with a passion that disregards even personal suffering and disadvantage.

I would not for a minute dispute this or write contemptuously about it. We in the West should regard it with the greatest respect, and we should remain sympathetic to the kind of worldwide Christianity it may well produce in coming decades. Many of us began our Christian pilgrimages in precisely the same kind of fervor and with a similar orientation. But neither should the fact of this religious tsunami headed in our direction incline us to deny that our own experience of salvation is now different from what it was nor cause us to disregard how the technological revolution of our culture actually compels us into a new and different mode of understanding our faith.

Judging by the polls of modern Americans' beliefs and practices, there is a much greater diversity of opinion about salvation even among the adherents of evangelicalism and fundamentalism than is evident from the confident, insistent voices of their leaders and authors. In 2005, for example, *Newsweek* magazine and Beliefnet questioned 1,004 Americans about their worship and beliefs. Some important statistics from that survey indicate that only 38 percent of respondents practice their religion today as they did while they were growing up. Only 39 percent said they practice their religion to forge a personal relationship with God, while 57 percent said they do it to help them be better persons, to find peace and happiness, or to connect with something larger than themselves. An astounding 68 percent of the evangelical Protestant respondents said they believe that a person who doesn't share their religious beliefs can go to heaven, while 83 percent of nonevangelical Protestants and 91 percent of Roman Catholics believed this.[25]

These figures indicate that a majority of American Christians, of whatever persuasion, are now far more open about their faith than their parents and grandparents were. And, while the fervent new Christianity that is sweeping Africa, Asia, and Central and South America is not so flexible and receptive to non-Christian beliefs and understanding, it is evident that most Western Christians, wherever one locates them along the spectrum of theological conservatism, are moving in an increasingly liberal direction.

If any further proof of this movement is necessary, it may well have been provided in the August 14, 2006, issue of *Newsweek* magazine, which featured a cover story about Billy Graham, the great lion of American evangelicalism, by religion editor Ron Meacham. It is called "Pilgrim's Progress."

No figure in conservative Christianity has been more widely accepted or revered than Graham. He has spoken to millions of people around the world, counseled U.S. presidents, and strongly and consistently represented the orthodox view of Christian evangelicalism, that there is no salvation outside of Jesus Christ.

Yet in this remarkable article, which describes an elder statesman quietly waiting to die and go to heaven, Graham admits that he has moved to a more centrist position in his faith, so that he regards both the religious right and the religious left as having gone to extremes. He says he regrets that he didn't get more theological training along his way. And he makes the astounding confession, "There are many things that I don't understand."

Now, after years of declaring, "The Bible says . . ." he admits that he no longer believes in the necessity of taking every verse of the Bible literally. "I'm not a literalist in the sense that every single jot and tittle is from the Lord," he says. "This is a little difference in my thinking through the years."

A little difference, indeed! It is actually a vast difference, a monumental difference, one that would have cast his entire ministry in a totally different light if he had arrived at it earlier.

Asked if he agrees with his son Franklin's announcement that the views of Muslims are "evil and wicked," he responds with startling frankness, "I'm sure there are many things that he and I are not in total agreement about."

"I spend more time on the love of God than I used to," he says. And obviously spending more time on the love of God has softened his position on just about everything from homosexuality and abortion to whether nonbelievers will have a place in heaven.

"A unifying theme of Graham's new thinking," says Meacham, "is humility. He is sure and certain of his faith in Jesus as the way to salvation. When asked whether heaven will be closed to good Jews, Muslims, Buddhists, Hindus, or secular people, though, Graham says: 'Those are decisions only the Lord will make. It would be foolish for me to speculate on who will be there and who won't . . . I believe the love of God is absolute. He said he gave his son for the whole world, and I think he loves everybody regardless of what label they have.'"

It may well upset some Christian hard-liners to hear this, continues Meacham, but in Billy Graham's opinion today "only God knows who is going to be saved."

Asked about her father's views, Anne Graham Lotz, who is also an evangelist, agreed that her father's position on things is different today because "the living of a life can soften your perspective."

If Billy Graham has changed this much in the last few years, it means that the whole world is changing.

The Inevitability of Change

Do I ever miss the simple, black-and-white version of Christianity shared with me as I was growing up? Only nostalgically, the way one misses the days when one believed in Santa Claus and the Easter Bunny. Then, it was all I knew. It was what my whole community believed and taught, and sometimes I miss the community itself, for it was, in general, a good and kind one in which to be reared. But no, I don't miss the old understandings of conversion and salvation, the idea that simply repenting of one's past and professing faith in Christ made a person a Christian and qualified him or her for everlasting life with God. It would have been nice if it were so. But it wasn't so then and it isn't so today.

Who was it — the ancient Greek philosopher Heraclitus? — who said that we can never step twice into the same river? Everything moves, shifts, changes. Even the cells in our own bodies totally reproduce themselves every seven years. Nothing about us is really the same in the different epochs of our lives — not our bodies, not our environments, and certainly not our minds and ways of looking at things.

Sometimes I wish the changes weren't so rapid. Nowadays they seem to occur with breathtaking speed. Since the electronic revolution began, culture is being transformed with exponential swiftness, not at the old, more comfortable rate. This is why fundamentalism is a world phenomenon in our time. Most people can't stand the pace of change, any more than they can bear to hurtle down the frighteningly precipitous inclines of giant roller coasters. Therefore they try to drive down stakes in the most essential part of their lives, their religions, and halt the progress — the *erosion,* they say — of everything.

I understand this, and sympathize. I would probably lock everything into a 1950s mode for the rest of my life if I could. But the Amish are a case in point that this is hard to do. As a people, they're now struggling with the question of whether they can use cell phones, inasmuch as cell phones don't require electrical lines running into their homes, the way conventional phones did. Their lives are always in tension between the past and the present, and they seem to be losing the battle to hold things where they were. There is even talk, around Lancaster, Pennsylvania, one of the most public Amish communities in the nation, of that group's relocating among the dairy farms of Wisconsin, where there would be less interface with the modern world.

I've already mentioned that new technological advances always send global culture into overdrive. It happened with fire, the axe, the wheel, metal ores, gunpowder, the printing press, the steam engine, electricity, the telephone, the airplane, and atomic power. But it has never happened with the speed that characterizes the revolution in electronic communications. The very instantaneity of e-communications is galvanizing everything in contemporary culture. There is almost nothing it doesn't affect. Medicine, philosophy, politics, manufacturing, merchandising, academics, the service industry — everything is changing swiftly and drastically.

"Computers have become part of the very fabric of creation," says Jennifer Cobb, an analyst of the digital revolution. In *Cybergrace,* she says, "Even now, those who never touch a computer personally — who don't use an ATM card or own a PC — are nonetheless surrounded by computer technology. Every time we pick up a phone, turn on the radio or television, get in our cars, climb on a bus, or go to the corner market for food, we participate in a world that is undergirded by a vast computerized system. The various types of computer systems that make up our world — from transportation to marketing to banking to communications — actually do the job they were designed to do remarkably well. They work. As a result, they are growing and becoming more powerful with each day."[26]

The complex cultural revolution taking place, says Cobb, isn't caused by technology in any simple sense. If we concluded this, we would be greatly oversimplifying "the dense interactions" between people and computers. Instead, she suggests, it may be more fitting to view the relationship between us and our tools as "a complex dance of becoming," in which our tools shape us as much as we shape them. Computer technology is forcing us to rethink our world. It even enlarges our wisdom. Then, with enhanced wisdom, we return to our tools and redesign them to do even more than they could do before. The dance goes on.

Think about the implications of this. Our reciprocity with the computer, with a machine we have made, is spiraling toward perfection and we are *both* changing. We make the computers smarter, and they make us smarter. And it is all happening at an incredible speed.

Technoculturist Ray Kurzweil, author of *The Singularity Is Near,* whom Bill Gates calls "the best person I know at preaching the future of artificial intelligence," says that we are now approaching *singularity,* the moment when artificial intelligence will have learned the patterns of human thought and be able to imitate them. It is staggering to consider what that moment will mean in the history of human understanding. Once computers have been programmed to reflect our own reasoning and emotive powers, they will be able to duplicate our efforts at thinking philosophically, solving complicated problems, creating works of art, writing books, designing buildings, and everything else we do, and will be able to do these things literally thousands of times faster than we can do them.[27]

When this moment is reached, the world is bound to change quickly and dramatically — even more quickly and dramatically than now. The computer may be able to point the way to instant peace in the Middle East. It may reveal how hunger and disease can be stamped out in Africa. Perhaps all the world's religions will be able to join in giant symposia and create a single religious understanding for the whole earth.

Kurzweil, who in the past has been remarkably successful at predicting when certain points in computer history would be reached, says that everything now points to the year 2045 as the time when singularity will occur. My grandchildren will be only middle-aged when that happens.

God of the Gaps?

Admittedly, it is sometimes tempting, given the vast changes occurring in one's own religious outlook and experiences, to agree with the skeptics that all religions are mere projections of how we would like things to be. Certainly it is harder to be persons of faith now than it was in the Middle Ages and most of the centuries leading up to our own. Then, things moved more slowly and there were fewer challenges from the philosophical and scientific opponents of religion. It was easier to believe when faith appeared to be universal.

Michael Polanyi, a philosopher of science and Fellow of the Royal Society of Great Britain, in *Science, Faith, and Society,* spoke of "the God of the gaps" — how human beings have always used enchantment or holiness to explain the mysteries of their lives. In primitive times, when there was no science, everything belonged to the realm of enchantment. People worshiped stones, rivers, trees, stars, the sun — literally anything that might possess a god or a demon. Then, when certain discoveries were made about the world and how it works — say, that gravity produces the rotation of planets around the sun — the world of enchantment shrank.

Today, with tremendous advances in medicine, astronomy, weather forecasting, brain science, and numerous other fields, that world has almost disappeared. God now appears to preside over very radically diminished mysteries in our existence, and we spend less time and energy trying to worship him.

But science is presently making a big U-turn on the subject of religion. Many of the most famous theoretical physicists of our time now speak of the mysteries of the universe as if they were far less simple than we were taught in our high school physics classes. In fact, those mysteries are so remarkable that some scientists admit they could not have come into existence without transcendent guidance.

Stephen Hawking's famous *A Brief History of Time,* for example, often sounds almost sacerdotal in its treatment of the search for a unified field theory that will explain both the general theory of relativity and quantum mechanics, which are presently at odds with one another. He even speaks of "the freedom of God" to choose how the world began, and to choose how he would begin again if the universe were to recollapse and form another infinite density.

Belief in God, says John Polkinghorne, another eminent British physicist and Anglican priest, may offer us the broadest possible way of coordinating our knowledge of many otherwise disjointed and unmanageable facts. "I believe," he writes in *Belief in God in an Age of Science,* "that those who are truly seeking an understanding through and through, and who will not settle for a facile and premature conclusion to that search, are seeking God, whether they acknowledge that divine quest or not. Theism is concerned with making *total* sense of the world."[28]

Total sense: that is the key to true spirituality in our age. And to do that, we must approach understanding not from outside everything else but from inside it, as participants in the great cosmic dance of electrically-charged particles. It is not something we shall come to in a lordly manner, as if we owned the universe; instead, it is what we shall discover by being an intimate part of everything, by viewing the universe from the merest corner of the action.

Diarmuid O'Murchu, a social psychologist, regards our situation from this beguiling perspective, and he sees it as leading to a new kind of spirituality in the future.

"Reclaiming our spiritual identity," he writes in *Quantum Theology,* "is not a case of becoming religious again, going to church on Sunday, following the rules and laws of a particular faith, reading the Bible or Koran everyday. No, it goes much deeper than any of this. As many of the great faiths suggest (but poorly implement) spirituality is about *enlightenment* and *liberation*. The spiritual journey is about opening up new horizons of love and understanding.... Our spiritual enlightenment is above all else a journey into the mystery of belonging where all is one, and the patriarchal dualisms and distinctions are seen for what they really are: destructive, controlling devices that fragment and alienate."[29]

What we need for discovering new pathways of salvation in our time is not retrenchment — retreating into the past to avoid the great changes washing over our culture and the way we think and behave — but the courage to go forward into a murky unknown, trusting that God, who has shown himself to our forebears in ways they could understand, will now reveal himself to us who possess new tools and methods by which to think and feel. We shall simply have to live for a while with uncertainty, as people always do in an age of transition. But in the end we shall be amply rewarded for the discomfort of this, because we shall see everything clearly again, and it will be as if a new heaven and a new earth had opened up before us.

Are we not saved in the meantime? Of course we are.

We must merely have faith and continue to grope our way to the future. That, after all, is the nature of salvation and what it is really about — not, as in the Old Testament, mere rescue from illness, enemies, or death, but, as in the New Testament, stepping out on promises, seeing redemption in unlikely places, committing ourselves to a way, not *out* of the woods, but *into* them.

I have a minister friend who has been through Job's own troubles. Several years ago, his youngest son accidentally killed his other son. Then the minister developed Parkinson's disease, possibly from the trauma of his child's death. When the disease affected his vocal chords, he had to stop being a minister because people had trouble understanding his public speech.

Recently, I received an e-mail in which he said he was at the lowest point "mentally, emotionally, physically, financially, and spiritually" he could ever recall, and for good reason:

- He had been out of his church for more than six months, and the salary extension he was granted had expired.

- He had been unable to find new work, even though he had tried.

- The disability pay he had been promised by social services was late in arriving.

- He could not find a new church where he was comfortable worshiping.

- He and his wife were separated and had begun divorce proceedings.

- Their remaining son had been institutionalized for drug addiction.

- His mother had recently died.

- His father had lung cancer.

- His father was afraid to stay alone at night, so he had been staying with him.

- His little dog had just been run over by a car.

- He had hurt his arm lifting a log.

Yet, in all this plethora of troubles, my friend did not despair. Instead, he hunkered down and wrote some of the most beautiful and eloquent memoirs I have ever seen. "It is as if I am losing everything piece by piece," he said, "but I am going to be okay."

He was one of the ministers I wrote to ask about his views on salvation. "Salvation," he responded, "is not a distant and shining phenomenon but a living and daily reality.... [It can come] from something so small, tender, unexpected, and vulnerable that it is hardly noticeable. God is the Creator of all things, yet he comes to us in smallness, weakness, and hiddenness. He comes to hear and respond to our cries for mercy, and he saves us. Yet we are still in the process of being saved, and the process depends on our response at every point along the way. In the end, it is what determines if we have lived and then died without having ever been affected by the beauty of wonder and the wonder of beauty."

Recently, this friend shared with me some letters he was e-mailing daily to his son, trying to encourage the son to trust God and learn to see his hand in the way our lives work. He also talked with his son about his Parkinson's disease, and how it was challenging him to find his own way again, just as the son was having to do. Here are some excerpts from those letters:

> "Faith is coming to the edge of the darkness and then taking another step."

> "You may feel as if life cannot go on the way it is, but the odd truth is that it can. The hope is that it will not remain that way. What is needed is a miracle. The miracle, my son, is to love life and feel good about it."

"I had a bad night last night. I woke up at 3 a.m. and couldn't turn over. I went through the alphabet, thinking of Bible verses beginning with A, B, C, and so on. Then I did the same with the first words of hymns. It is amazing how long you can pray when you can do nothing else."

[He told his son about a time when he spent twenty-one days as a guest in a Trappist monastery, where no speech was allowed. It was very hard at first, he said.] "But once I pressed on, it was as if my entire being adjusted to the rhythm of my surroundings."

"Everything seems so hopeless and my spirit is so low. Then I begin to notice that the darkness is not empty. There is a sense of presence, and it is friendly. It is the infinite, awesome Creator God. Then there is Christ's gentle command, 'Take my hand.' I do, and then the once silent music audibly fills all the space around me and the Spirit moves ever so slowly to the music, drawing my whole being into the dance of the dark. And I am comforted and not alone."

My friend's incredible attitude and beautiful words made me think of the flowering trees in Africa that drop their fragrant blossoms on the ground, so that, trodden under foot, their sweet aroma perfumes everything for a great distance.

Had my friend known only the salvation of the ancient world — that described by the Greeks and Hebrews — he might have written a poem asking God for deliverance, as the psalmists so often did:

In you, O Lord, I take refuge;
  let me never be put to shame.
In your righteousness deliver me and rescue me;
  incline your ear to me and save me.

                              (Psalm 71:1–2)

To you, O Lord, I call;
  my rock, do not refuse to hear me,
for if you are silent to me,
  I shall be like those who go down to the Pit.

                              (Psalm 28:1)

As a deer longs for flowing streams,
  so my soul longs for you, O God.
My soul thirsts for God,
  for the living God.
When shall I come and behold
  the face of God?
My fears have been my food day and night,
  while people say to me continually,
    "Where is your God?"   (Psalm 42:1–3)

But my friend's salvation is much more than this. It is hope, originally revealed to him in Christ, that God is still there whenever we suffer and does not vanish like the frost at noontime. It is trust that he himself will be able to perdure, and, having done so, to find his composure again. Not only that, but he will be wiser and stronger for having endured the things that have happened to him. And even more, he shall continue to belong to God for all eternity, through this life and whatever lies beyond it.

That is the hope I share with him. I do not understand the hope. I do not even understand myself, or the world in which I live. And I cannot begin to describe the *mysterium tremendum et fascinans* that is God. It is all far, far beyond my limited powers of reason and explanation.

Yet I know that I am saved, in some inexplicable way, from everything that threatens me most deeply: both earthly distress and eternal nothingness. How did Luther's great hymn put it?

And though this world, with devils filled, should threaten
        to undo us,
we will not fear, for God hath willed his truth to triumph
        through us.
The Prince of Darkness grim, we tremble not for him;
his rage we can endure, for lo, his doom is sure;
one little word shall fell him.[30]

It would be hard to say it better, even in an age of quantum physics and depth psychology. I doubt if our computers, in the day of singularity, will be able to improve upon it. It isn't a salvation merely *from* something — our troubles, our ineptitude, our fragility and limitation — but a salvation *to* something. To belief without too fine a point on it. To a sense of belonging, both to God and to our wider humanity. And to an outcome yet to be determined, beyond everything we know of this life and the world.

I cannot prove it, of course. But I do not feel the need to prove it, for I am no longer anxious about the salvation of others. No more testimonies under naked light bulbs to young men clad solely in jeans or to migrant workers in the saloon district of a Southern city. The same love that is caring for me will care for them. We are all in it together, even if the others do not realize this.

The God named Love is working it out. Perhaps, in his mind, it is already worked out.

A Final Word

This final word — a summary — though it is actually three ideas:

First, God is God, and God is the arbiter of salvation, not we. Sometimes we forget that, in our anxiety to find protection from the vicissitudes of life and death. The Bible rarely forgets it. It is God who initiates human salvation, not the Israelites and not the early Christians, and it is God who finally consummates it. This is why Paul always insisted on our remembering that we are saved by *grace*, not by works, and why Luther picked up the same cry in the days of Reformation.

It is why, beyond every other reason I can imagine, Calvin bent his efforts to devise a super theology built on the single notion of the sovereignty of God, and, child despiser that he was, insisted that it was within God's divine prerogative to decide which children would be saved and which would go to hell. (In Calvin's defense, children were not the natural objects of affection in his day that they became after the publication of Charles Dickens's novels in the mid-nineteenth century.) And it may even explain why certain fundamentalists today, such as Pat Robertson and Jerry Falwell, make some of the embarrassing comments they do about God's having sent such events as 9/11 and Hurricane Katrina as punishments for sin. The comments are often out of bounds, but the intention, seen in the best light, is to glorify God, who is, after all, the giver of salvation.

៹

Second, because it is God who effects our salvation, and not we ourselves, our methods of seeking salvation, sometimes natural and sometimes ingenious, don't really matter all that much. The Hebrews did it by a sacrificial system, which, at its finest, needed a temple and a hierarchy of priests. In Jesus' time, the scribes and Pharisees, given a despoiled temple and the presence of pagans on their doorsteps, created a system that effectively bypassed the temple, in a campaign for holy living, which Jesus plainly regarded as oppressive and ungodly.

The early Christians, seizing on the Jewish nostalgia for the *mythos* of sacrifice, preached Jesus as the sacrificial lamb par excellence. The early and medieval churches developed this theme into an elaborate sacramental system, and they eventually crowned it with the doctrine of transubstantiation, declaring that the bread and wine on the altar became the Savior's actual body and blood. The Reformers, retaining the Pauline emphasis on Jesus' sacrifice but rejecting the notion of transubstantiation, made faith in Christ's achievement the cornerstone of their doctrinal house.

And on and on it has gone, and will go, with each generation offering its own particular twist on the methodology of redemption.

But if God is the one who saves, and it is God who initiates and sustains the program of salvation, whatever it is, then doesn't

it stand to reason that the methodology itself isn't all that important? It only serves, in the end, to paint God as an arbitrary
divinity, one who insists that human beings fulfill their contract
with him, dotting all the i's and crossing all the t's, in order to give
them the salvation they so desperately or not-so-desperately seek.
Does this really preserve the sovereignty of God? Or does it make
God look like a sicko parent who fulfills his own control needs
by establishing a series of obstacles for his devotees to negotiate
before he rewards them for their trouble?

We have learned to spot anthropomorphisms when someone
talks about God in human terms, as though he actually had arms,
legs, eyes, and ears. Why can't we see that systems of salvation
can also be anthropomorphic, formed in the images of the games
we play as human beings?

This becomes threatening to most of our religious systems, of
course, not only because it makes them appear less important than
we have believed them to be but because it also opens the gate
to the anthropomorphic systems of other religions such as Islam,
Buddhism, and Hinduism. Do we really want to admit that God
might not reject people from these other systems because they
don't eagerly leap over the hurdles we have devised in our own
Judeo-Christian tradition?

Heavens! That might also allow for agnostics and free thinkers,
for all those skeptical people who have withheld their support for
religions of any kind, not wanting to surrender their autonomy
to organized cults and sect groups, and that would be religious
anarchy, wouldn't it? There wouldn't be any control of any kind.
We would have to leave it all in the hands of God.

Which, if I remember correctly, is where we said it was in the beginning. Ah, well.

⤳

Third, if salvation is still, as it has always been, in God's hands, and if the methodology is of little consequence because it *is* in the hands of God, then salvation is finally not even dependent on our acceptance or rejection of it. God will save us whether we accept it or not.

Except.

Now I am going to say something that may redeem me the teensy-weensyest bit with those who have decided that I am a hopeless heretic.

⤳

The exception is this: *acceptance is important to us.*

Something extremely important happens to us when we realize that God loves us and is already in the process of redeeming us.

If the scientists who are now doing such clever things to photograph chemical changes occurring in the brain could take a picture of what happens when it suddenly dawns on a person that the Creator of the Universe truly cares about him or her and is moving heaven and earth to help that person not only survive but flourish amid the various forces impinging on us, I believe they would see a startlingly dramatic transformation occur. There might be a flash of brilliant red to signal a sudden burst of self-confidence that wasn't there before, or a gradual pooling of greens and blues to indicate a new peacefulness and relaxation, or a lovely splotch of magenta to mark the birth of a fresh sense of community with the rest of the world. Whatever the color and nature of the transformation, it would signal an essential turning point in the person's life, a moment of transfiguration that some would understand as conversion or new birth.

This alone is worth a continued effort at evangelizing the world — not to count converts like scalps hanging from our belts or to pride ourselves in our dominance on the mission fields, but to help people everywhere and in every culture to find the switches that turn on the best that is inside them, saving the world from the selfishness and prejudices and divisions that now cripple and destroy it, and turning our planet into a holiday scene of bright lights going on in everybody, with everybody coming out into the streets to dance and sing and celebrate love.

That, after all, is the truly communal nature of salvation — not collecting in little enclaves and whispering among ourselves that we are the best and ours is the only way to God, but embracing and celebrating and being generous with everyone because this is the nature of God and the angels.

Party, anyone?

Notes

1. Johannes Pedersen, *Israel: Its Life and Culture* (London: Oxford University Press, 1959), 462.

2. Jacob Neusner, *An Introduction to Judaism* (Louisville: Westminster John Knox Press, 1991), 134.

3. H. H. Rowley, in *The Faith of Israel* (London: SCM Press, 1956), says there is no real evidence in the psalms of faith in a life after death, but there are "reachings out after such a faith" (175).

4. Ibid.

5. Ibid., 167.

6. George Foot Moore, *Judaism in the First Centuries of the Christian Era* (Cambridge, MA: Harvard University Press, 1954), 500.

7. Reynolds Price, *A Whole New Life* (New York: Penguin Books, 1995), 32.

8. Ibid., 43.

9. Ibid., 39.

10. Ibid., 76.

11. Ralph G. Wilburn, *The Historical Shape of Faith* (Louisville: Westminster John Knox Press, 1966), 17.

12. Martin Dibelius, *Paul*, ed. Georg Kümmel, trans. Frank Clarke (Philadelphia: Westminster Press, 1953), 107–8.

13. For a larger discussion of Paul's syncretism, see Rudolf Bultmann, *Primitive Christianity in Its Contemporary Setting*, trans. R. H. Fuller (New York: Living Age Books, 1957), 162–79.

14. Eric C. Rust, *Salvation History* (Louisville: Westminster John Knox Press, 1962), 99.

15. See Walter Brueggemann, *Theology of the Old Testament* (Minneapolis: Fortress Press, 1997), 729.

16. For a full collection of these documents, see James M. Robinson, ed., *The Nag Hammadi Library in English* (San Francisco: HarperCollins, 1988).

17. Elizabeth Lesser, *The New American Spirituality: A Seeker's Guide* (New York: Random House, 1999), 51–52.

18. Kenneth Woodward, "Pilgrimage in an Age of World Religions," unpublished lecture at Guilford College, Greensboro, North Carolina, November 2005.

19. Harvey Cox, *Many Mansions: A Christian's Encounter with Other Faiths* (Boston: Beacon Press, 1988), 121.

20. Wade Clark Roof, *Spiritual Marketplace: Baby Boomers and the Remaking of American Religion* (Princeton, NJ: Princeton University Press, 1999), 62.

21. J. P. Scholfield, copyright Robert Coleman, 1939.

22. David Steindl-Rast, *Gratefulness, the Heart of Prayer* (Mahwah, NJ: Paulist Press, 1984), 21–22.

23. James Hillman, *The Soul's Code: In Search of Character and Calling* (New York: Random House, 1996), 4–5.

24. Philip Jenkins, "The Next Christianity," *Atlantic Monthly* (October 2002), 54.

25. "In Search of the Spiritual," *Newsweek,* September 5, 2005, 46–64.

26. Jennifer Cobb, *Cybergrace: The Search for God in the Digital World* (New York: Crown Books, 1998), 18–19.

27. Ray Kurzweil, *The Singularity Is Near: When Humans Transcend Biology* (New York: Viking Press, 2005).

28. John Polkinghorne, *Belief in God in an Age of Science* (New Haven, CT: Yale University Press, 1998), 24.

29. Diarmuid O'Murchu, *Quantum Theology* (New York: Crossroad, 2000), 77.

30. Martin Luther, "A Mighty Fortress Is Our God."

Bibliography

Armstrong, Karen. *A History of God.* New York: Ballantine Books, 1993.

Augustine. *Confessions.* Trans. Henry Chadwick. Oxford: Oxford University Press, 1991.

Benedetto of Mantua. *The Benefits of Christ's Death.* Trans. Edward Courtenay. Revised R. W. Johnson. Cambridge, England: Dughton, Bell & Co., 1855.

Bettenson, Henry, ed. *Documents of the Christian Church.* New York: Oxford University Press, 1956.

———. *The Early Christian Fathers.* New York: Oxford University Press, 1956.

Brueggemann, Walter. *Theology of the Old Testament.* Minneapolis: Fortress Press, 1997.

Bultmann, Rudolf. *Primitive Christianity in Its Contemporary Setting.* Trans. R. H. Fuller. New York: Living Age Books, 1957.

Cobb, Jennifer. *Cybergrace: The Search for God in the Digital World.* New York: Crown Books, 1998.

Cox, Harvey. *Many Mansions: A Christian's Encounter with Other Faiths.* Boston: Beacon Press, 1988.

Cullmann, Oscar. *Immortality of the Soul or Resurrection of the Dead? The Witness of the New Testament.* London: Epworth Press, 1958.

Dibelius, Martin. *Paul.* Edited and completed by Werner Georg Kümmel. Trans. Frank Clarke. Philadelphia: Westminster Press, 1953.

Dunne, John. *The Way of All the Earth.* New York: Macmillan, 1972.

Eck, Diana L. *A New Religious America.* San Francisco: HarperCollins, 2001.

Fuller, Robert C. *Spiritual but Not Religious: Understanding Unchurched America.* New York: Oxford University Press, 2001.

Hawking, Stephen. *A Brief History of Time.* New York: Bantam Books, 1990.

Hick, John, ed. *The Myth of God Incarnate.* Philadelphia: Westminster Press, 1977.

Hillman, James. *The Soul's Code: In Search of Character and Calling.* New York: Random House, 1996.

Ignatius of Loyola. *Spiritual Exercises.* New York: Paulist Press, 1991.

"In Search of the Spiritual." *Newsweek,* September 5, 2005.

Jenkins, Philip. "The Next Christianity." *Atlantic Monthly* (October 2002).

Kerr, Hugh T., and John Mulder, eds. *Conversions: The Christian Experience.* Grand Rapids: William B. Eerdmans, 1989.

Küng, Hans. *On Being a Christian.* Trans. Edward Quinn. New York: Doubleday, 1984.

Kurzweil, Ray. *The Singularity Is Near: When Humans Transcend Biology.* New York: Viking Press, 2005.

Laing, R. D. *The Politics of Experience.* New York: Pantheon/Random House, 1967.

Latourette, Kenneth Scott. *A History of Christianity.* New York: Harper-Collins, 1953.

Lesser, Elizabeth. *The New American Spirituality: A Seeker's Guide.* New York: Random House, 1999.

Lewis, C. S. *Surprised by Joy.* New York: Harcourt/Harvest, 1995.

Lewis, Hywel D. *The Self and Immortality.* London: Macmillan Press, 1973.

Lotz, David W. *Altered Landscapes: Christianity in America, 1935–1985.* Grand Rapids: William B. Eerdmans, 1989.

Maas, Robin, and Gabriel O'Donnell. *Spiritual Traditions for the Contemporary Church.* Nashville: Abingdon Press, 1990.

Moore, George Foot. *Judaism in the First Centuries of the Christian Era.* Cambridge, MA: Harvard University Press, 1954.

Muggeridge, Malcolm. *Jesus Rediscovered.* New York: Doubleday, 1969.

Neill, Stephen. *Christian Faith and Other Faiths: The Christian Dialogue with Other Religions.* New York: Oxford University Press, 1970.

Neusner, Jacob. *An Introduction to Judaism.* Louisville: Westminster John Knox Press, 1991.

O'Murchu, Diarmuid. *Quantum Theology.* New York: Crossroad, 2000.

Pedersen, Johannes. *Israel: Its Life and Culture.* London: Oxford University Press, 1959.

Pelikan, Jaroslav. *The Excellent Empire: The Fall of Rome and the Triumph of the Church.* San Francisco: HarperCollins, 1987.

Polkinghorne, John. *Belief in God in an Age of Science.* New Haven, CT: Yale University Press, 1998.

Price, Reynolds. *A Whole New Life.* New York: Penguin Books, 1995.

Redfield, James, Michael Murphy, and Sylvia Timbers. *God and the Evolving Universe.* New York: Tarcher/Putnam, 2003.

Riley, Gregory. *The River of God: A New History of Origins.* New York: HarperCollins, 2001.

Robinson, James M., ed. *The Nag Hammadi Library in English.* San Francisco: HarperCollins, 1988.

Roof, Wade Clark. *Spiritual Marketplace: Baby Boomers and the Remaking of American Religion.* Princeton, NJ: Princeton University Press, 1999.

Rowley, H. H. *The Faith of Israel.* London: SCM Press, 1956.

Rust, Eric C. *Salvation History.* Louisville: Westminster John Knox Press, 1962.

Spong, John Shelby. *A New Christianity for a New Age.* San Francisco: HarperCollins, 2001.

Steindl-Rast, David. *Gratefulness, the Heart of Prayer.* Mahwah, NJ: Paulist Press, 1984.

Walker, Williston. *A History of the Christian Church.* New York: Charles Scribner's Sons, 1970.

Weiss, Johannes. *Earliest Christianity.* Trans. and ed. Frederick C. Grant. 2 vols. New York: HarperCollins, 1959.

Wilburn, Ralph G. *The Historical Shape of Faith.* Louisville: Westminster John Knox Press, 1966.

Wolfson, Harry A. *The Philosophy of the Church Fathers.* Cambridge, MA: Harvard University Press, 1956.

Woodward, Kenneth. "Pilgrimage in an Age of World Religions." Unpublished lecture at Guilford College, Greensboro, North Carolina. November 2005.

Wuthnow, Robert. *Christianity in the 21st Century.* New York: Oxford University Press, 1993.

Acknowledgments

Acknowledging the people responsible for a book is a lot like Oscar speeches in Hollywood: the list could go on and on. In a book like this one, it would obviously include the important figures in one's life, both early and late, who have contributed so much to who one has become — in this case, the ministers and other church figures of my youth, the teachers I learned from, the colleagues with whom I exchanged ideas, the authors of all the books I read, and the friends and acquaintances who have done so much to shape my existence across the years. And it goes without saying that it would also include the members of my immediate family — my beautiful wife Anne and our sons Eric and Krister — with whom my relationships have been so symbiotic that I would not recognize myself apart from them.

But for this particular book, I owe a special word of thanks to the Senior Editor of The Crossroad Publishing Company, Roy M. Carlisle, along with John Jones, Editorial Director, who said that they and the staff at Crossroad thought it was time for me to write a book about salvation and, when Roy had finished reading the manuscript, pronounced it a book that only I could have written.

In the often impersonal, business-oriented world of publishing, this is the kind of thoughtful, encouraging relationship that is all too frequently missing. So to Roy and John, and to Crossroad's lovely CEO, Gwendolin Herder, and all the amiable, hard-working staff members who make Crossroad a unique press for a time like this, I say thank you and God bless you for providing me with the opportunity to write a book it had not even occurred to me to write!

About the Author

John Killinger has had a distinguished career as a churchman, professor, and author. Holder of a Ph.D. in theology from Princeton University and another Ph.D. in literature from the University of Kentucky, he taught preaching, worship, and literature at Vanderbilt Divinity School from 1965 to 1980. He has also taught as a visiting professor at the University of Chicago, City College of New York, Princeton Seminary, and Claremont School of Theology, and was Distinguished Professor of Religion and Culture at Samford University in Birmingham, Alabama.

Ordained as a Baptist minister at the age of eighteen, he left teaching for a decade in the 1980s to be senior minister of the First Presbyterian Church in Lynchburg, Virginia. He then became senior minister of the First Congregational Church of Los Angeles, the oldest English-speaking congregation in that city. Since leaving Samford University in 1996 he has also served as minister of the Little Stone Church on Mackinac Island, Michigan.

Dr. Killinger has written more than fifty books, on subjects ranging from Hemingway and the Theater of the Absurd to prayers, preaching, and biblical commentary as well as fiction.

He has also served on the editorial boards of *Christian Ministry*, *Pulpit Digest*, and the Library of Distinctive Sermons.

John and his wife, Anne (also an author), love reading, writing, travel, theater, and hiking. Their rambling home is on the outskirts of Warrenton, Virginia, halfway between the nation's capital and the Blue Ridge Mountains.

A Word
from the Editor

Salvation. Life. Abundant Life. Death. Eternal Death. A serious
word, salvation, with serious implications for all individuals according to theologians and preachers. But all I can think of is its
use in a song by Neil Diamond, "Brother Love's Traveling Salvation Show." The lyrics of that song make it very clear that in
a consumer culture like ours (USA) all we can really imagine
is that salvation is about buying something or receiving benefits. Or being "saved" from something, even if we are not quite
sure what.

As my friend Lori likes to say, "We have been shortchanged by
conservative churches peddling salvation benefits like they were
parcels on a Monopoly board, and we get to live in a heavenly
'mansion.'" She is right of course. On the other hand, our more
progressive churches can only imagine salvation as an earthly
peace in the here and now, with everyone being nice. There is
nothing very compelling about those benefits either, frankly. I
will grant that there are certain megachurches that have been
able to package these salvation benefits in a way that is appealing

to suburban shoppers. You might have noticed that megachurches are never in the midst of diverse urban locales with any issues of poverty, racism, and multi-culturalism. These large churches are usually situated in suburban sprawl where all of life is oriented around homogeneous neighbors, a false sense of safety, and shopping malls. Church is just one more place to "shop" and to escape those scary cities.

Most churches have been declining for years because no one cares about these conservative or progressive "benefits" when more people are trapped in poverty than ever before, or when wages and salaries for the middle class have stagnated for years, or when elected officials lie about international terrorism and engage in preemptive wars, or when most churches can only seem to bore you to tears on a Sunday morning, or finally, when you are looking for meaning in the face of mortality and no one has anything profound to say. This is not to deny that we are a nation of people who "believe" and who care about our spirituality. We most definitely do, and all of the surveys and polls confirm that fact. The trouble is that it doesn't seem to make much difference in people's lives. We really do need to understand this notion of salvation anew.

Indeed, this is where Dr. Killinger provides a service that is invaluable. By introducing us to the various notions of salvation that have emerged throughout the history of the church he gives us a chance to rethink our own notion of it. And by guiding us through the Old and New Testaments he gives us a foundation for thinking about this serious word, salvation, in a way that is not limited by personal opinion or faddish turns.

Salvation is a serious word. I believe that with all of my heart. Which is why we need this book, why we need to read it carefully and think about our own mortality. Finally someone does have something profound to say about it. Maybe this book will enable us to listen to the deepest whispers of our own hearts and name what we are longing for. I hope so.

Roy M. Carlisle
Senior Editor

Of Related Interest

Peter Feuerherd
HOLY LAND USA
A Catholic Ride Through America's
Evangelical Landscape

In *Holy Land USA*, Peter Feuerherd, respected Catholic journalist and commentator, uses his own family and professional experiences as a starting point for an entertaining look at evangelical culture in America. Instead of offering more theories and theologies, Feuerherd helps us meet evangelicals face to face, interviewing people, famous and not, who open a window into the beliefs, daily lives, and actions of this significant and growing part of the American landscape.

Topics include:

- Church Bible study fellowships
- Catholic art
- Passion Plays
- liturgy
- college and seminary training
- views of salvation
- the Bible

0-8245-2297-4, paperback

crossroad

Also by John Killinger

TEN THINGS I LEARNED WRONG
FROM A CONSERVATIVE CHURCH

John Killinger warmly relates the story of his salvation from an abusive father by the kindly people of his local Baptist church in rural Kentucky. Part memoir, part theological reflection, this story will be of help to many who wish to remain faithful to the Lord, but struggle with the strict tenets of biblical fundamentalism. With gentle humor and compassion, Killinger shows us how faith is a constant, even as our beliefs and the world around us change

0-8245-2011-4, paperback

SEVEN THINGS THEY DON'T TEACH YOU
IN SEMINARY

John Killinger, author of *Ten Things I Learned Wrong from a Conservative Church*, offers this insightful, very honest, and sometimes humorous look at the most important things all seminarians need to know — and aren't learning in seminary. Topics include: Churches Are Institutions, Not Centers of Spirituality; Appearance over Reality; Drowning in a Sea of Minutiae; Pastoral Search Committees; Preaching Sunday after Sunday; Mean Church Members; The Calling to Be a Minister; The Ten Commandments for a Truly Successful Ministry

0-8245-2392-X, paperback

crossroad

Also by John Killinger

WINTER SOULSTICE
Celebrating the Spirituality of the Wisdom Years

John Killinger has long been a trusted voice and elder statesman for mainstream American Christians. In this extended
meditation, Dr. Killinger shows how age gives us a richer
understanding of the different aspects of our lives — memories, ambitions, work, conflicts, and even sex. True spiritual
growth occurs when we see our memories and experiences,
our choices and failures to choose, our friendships and as-
sociations, come together like the streams of a river to form
the spiritual beings we have become.

0-8245-2316-4, paperback

Please support your local bookstore,
or call 1-800-707-0670 for Customer Service.

For a free catalog, write us at

THE CROSSROAD PUBLISHING COMPANY
16 Penn Plaza – 481 Eighth Avenue, Suite 1550
New York, NY 10001

Visit our website at
www.crossroadpublishing.com
All prices subject to change.

crossroad